THE PARENTS' GUIDE TO
THE NATIONAL CURRICULUM

A GUIDE FOR PARENTS

Charles Hymas

Chapmans Publishers
A Division of the Orion Publishing Group Ltd
5 Upper St Martin's Lane
London WC2H 9EA

To Sarah and Katharine

First published by Chapmans 1993

© Charles Hymas 1993

The right of Charles Hymas to be identified as the author of this work has been asserted by him in accordance with the Copyright, Designs and Patents Act, 1988

ISBN 1-85592-696-2

All rights reserved
No part of this publication may be reproduced, stored in a retrieval system, or transmitted, in any form or by any means without the prior permission in writing of the publishers, nor be otherwise circulated in any form of binding or cover other than that in which it is published and without a similar condition including this condition being imposed on the subsequent purchaser.

Designed and typeset on an Apple Macintosh by
Sasha Kennedy (ACE Ltd)
Printed and bound in Great Britain by
Butler & Tanner Ltd, Frome and London

Contents

Preface		IV

1 A Basic Guide to the National Curriculum and Tests — 1

What Is the National Curriculum? — 1
How Does the National Curriculum Work? — 2
How is My Child Tested? — 3

2 What Your Child Will Study at Primary School — 5

The National Curriculum for Children Aged Five to 11 — 5
English (Reading, Writing, Speaking and Listening) — 5
Mathematics — 12
Science — 14
The Foundation Subjects — 16
Teaching Methods in Primary Schools — 18

3 What Your Child Will Study at Secondary School — 19

The National Curriculum for Pupils Aged 11 to 16 — 19
How Secondary Schools Organise Their Teaching — 20
English — 22
Mathematics — 23
Science — 24
Modern Foreign Languages — 26
Technology — 27
The Other Foundation Subjects — 28
How Can You Help Your Child at Secondary School? — 29

4 Choices at 14 and Beyond — 31

Choices for 14-Year-Olds — 31
Vocational Qualifications — 32
Choices for 16-Year-Olds — 33
A-Levels — 33
Vocational Qualifications — 34

5 Tests and Examinations — 39

Methods of Testing at Seven, 11 and 14 — 39
Methods of Testing at 15 or 16 — 40
National Tests at Seven, 11 and 14 — 40
Tests for Seven-Year-Olds — 40
Tests for 11-Year-Olds — 48
Tests for 14-Year-Olds — 55
The GCSE — 56
A-Levels — 58

6 Choosing a School — 61

What Sort of Schools Are There? — 61
What to Look for in a Good School — 62
Choosing a Primary School — 63
Choosing a Secondary School — 66

7 Parents' Rights — 71

School Reports — 71
Going Grant-Maintained? — 73
The Right to Complain — 73
Expulsions from School — 74
Charging and Benefits — 74
Religious Education and Acts of Collective Worship — 75

8 Special Options — 77

Children with Special Educational Needs — 77
Music — 78
Art — 79
Physical Education and Sport — 80
Technology — 81
Specialist State Schools — 81
Able or Gifted Children — 81

Reading Lists for English — 82

Glossary — 85

Preface

The National Curriculum Review 1993

The introduction of a national curriculum for all schools is the most important change in British education since the Second World War. Its principal aim is to raise standards by defining the knowledge and skills that all children should be taught.

The guidelines for each subject in the national curriculum were completed in 1992. However, it was clear by then that the curriculum was too bureaucratic and over-prescriptive.

In primary schools, teachers said that the content specified for the nine subjects that they had to teach was so great that it was limiting the time they could devote to the basics of reading, writing and arithmetic. In secondary schools, it was threatening to squeeze out other subjects such as extra foreign language teaching, the classics and vocational courses.

The national tests that pupils have to sit at the ages of seven, 11 and 14 were also too cumbersome and took up too much time.

Government ministers, therefore, announced a review of the curriculum and tests in spring 1993. The preliminary results of that review were published in August 1993. Many of the changes recommended by the review group of education experts are unlikely to take place until at least autumn 1994.

Recommendations

The aim of the review is to sweep away the bureaucracy associated with the curriculum and the tests. By slimming down the guidelines that specify what teachers should teach, it is intended that schools should have more time to devote both to the basics and to other subjects and activities outside the curriculum.

The Primary School Curriculum: For pupils aged five to seven in the first Key Stage of their education, the review proposes that teachers should have more time to concentrate on teaching the basics of English (reading and writing) and mathematics by reducing the amount that has to be covered in the other subjects. There are seven other subjects that also have to be taught: science, technology, history, geography, art, music and PE. The content specified in guidelines for each of these will be substantially reduced. It is intended that the national curriculum should take up no more than 85 to 90 per cent of a teacher's class time.

For pupils aged eight to 11 in the second Key Stage of their education, the nine subjects will remain compulsory, with English, mathematics and science given the most time. However, the national curriculum will be pruned so that it takes up no more than 80 to 85 per cent of a school's timetable. The extra time should give schools the chance to introduce other subjects such as foreign languages, which are not at present compulsory in primary schools.

The Secondary School Curriculum: Pupils aged 11 to 14 will have to study the nine subjects plus a foreign language. Again, the content specified in the curriculum will be reduced so that up to a quarter of a school's timetable can be devoted to other subjects and activities.

The biggest changes are mooted for pupils aged 14 to 16, who are studying for their GCSEs. For all pupils, English, mathematics and science will remain compulsory and the study of a foreign language and some technology will probably be required. However, beyond those subjects, the review suggests that there may be some scope for more flexibility in pupils' choice of subjects from options including history, geography, additional foreign languages, the arts and vocational courses (designed to prepare children for the world of work).

National Tests at Seven, 11 and 14: Seven-year-olds will sit national tests set by outside examiners in only English and mathematics in the summer of 1994. Unlike previous years, pupils' ability in science will be assessed by teachers as part of their day-to-day classroom work rather than through externally-set national tests. The English and mathematics tests will concentrate on the basics of reading, spelling and arithmetic (addition, subtraction, multiplication and division).

The tests for 11-year-olds in English, mathematics and science will be a national pilot in the summer of 1994. This means that it will be up to individual schools to decide whether to take part. The tests will be compulsory in summer 1995.

Fourteen-year-olds will sit national tests in English, mathematics and science in summer 1994. These will be externally set, written papers lasting a total of six and three-quarter hours. The English test will include a paper on a Shakespeare play that will have to be taken by pupils judged to be Level 4 or above in the national curriculum (see page 3 for an explanation of these levels).

Children's results in the national tests for 14-year-olds will be reported to parents separately from teachers' internal assessments of children's progress in the subjects. Consultations are to be carried out to see whether national tests for 14-year-olds should be marked by external examiners rather than by children's teachers. This is seen as one way of easing the administrative workload and bureaucracy for teachers.

Changing the Grades: The review canvasses the possibility that the ten-level grading scale against which each child's progress is measured should be replaced (see page 3). One alternative could be to have five grades for children at each of the ages of seven, 11 and 14. Pupils judged to be of average ability would get the middle grade (possibly a C), with two grades above for brighter children and two grades below for less able pupils. Decisions about such a change will not be taken until early in 1994.

The Timescale: The government's advisers responsible for the review of the national curriculum have yet to decide whether to revise the guidelines for all the subjects at once, or to reform them one subject at a time. Whatever approach is adopted, the changes to what children are taught are unlikely to take place in the country's classrooms until September 1995. Final decisions about the future shape of the curriculum will not be taken until early in 1994.

The English and technology curricula are already being revised. The new English curriculum places more emphasis on the phonic approach to teaching reading (see page 6) and on the teaching of grammar, and for the first time it details a list of authors that children should study (see pages 82–84). It also requires higher standards from pupils to achieve particular levels. The technology curriculum lays greater stress on practical tasks.

The Education Act (1993)

The Education Act (1993) makes substantial changes to the way that schools are organised in England and Wales. The changes will start to take effect from September 1993.

New Funding Agencies will be set up through the Act to distribute money to grant-maintained schools. These are schools that have opted out of their local authority's control and at present receive their funds direct from the government. In England, the agency will be known as the Funding Agency for Schools (FAS). In Wales, it will be known as the Schools Funding Council for Wales.

When 10 per cent of the pupils in an area are being educated in grant-maintained schools, the agencies will share responsibility with the local education authority for providing school places. Once more than 75 per cent of pupils in an education authority are in grant-maintained schools, the agencies will take on full responsibility for ensuring that there are sufficient school places in the area.

There are so far only a few authorities where 10 per cent of pupils are educated in grant-maintained schools. However, in some smaller authorities, it may require only a handful of schools to become grant-maintained for the agency to come into operation. Like a local authority, it will have powers to propose the closure of schools, extensions and the creation of new schools.

Going Grant-Maintained: All schools' governing bodies will be required each year to consider whether to become grant-maintained. Parents will be told the outcome of these deliberations in the school's annual report. The Act also makes it easier for schools to become grant-maintained, limits the amount of money that local authorities can spend on campaigns and allows small primary schools to opt out together as a group and then be managed jointly by a single governing body.

Special Teams of Educational Experts can be appointed by the secretary of state for education to take over the running of a school if it has been judged by inspectors to be 'failing'. These teams will be known as Education Associations. After their period of control, the school will either close or become grant-maintained.

A New Independent Tribunal will be set up to hear appeals from parents against local education authority decisions about the education of children with special needs. The tribunals will replace local appeals committees. There will also be a new code of practice for the education of children with special needs and a right for parents of children with 'statements' of their special needs to state a preference for a state school of their choice (see page 77 for what a statement means).

Other Changes include powers for the secretary of state for education to submit his own plans for closing down schools with surplus places and have his proposals referred to a public inquiry.

There will also be the creation of a new authority to oversee the national curriculum and tests, and to advise the government. It will be known as the School Curriculum and Assessment Authority (SCAA), and takes over from the National Curriculum Council and the School Examinations and Assessment Council.

Voluntary bodies and parents will be able to apply to establish their own grant-maintained schools if they are willing to find 15 per cent of the cost.

Sex education is made a separate, compulsory subject but parents will have a right to withdraw their children from lessons in the subject.

Acknowledgements

Finally, I am grateful to the following for permission to reproduce questions from the 1993 tests and pilot tests for seven, 11 and 14 year-olds: page 42 (top), © Crown Copyright; pages 42–47, © Copyright Controller HMSO, from *Standard Assessment Task: Pupil and Source Sheet Booklet*; pages 48–52, from University of Leeds/SEAC; pages 53–54, © Crown Copyright, produced by CRIPSAT and UCLES under contract to SEAC.

Charles Hymas,
The Sunday Times,
August 1993

1
A Basic Guide to the National Curriculum and Tests

Why Is There a National Curriculum?

The Education Reform Act of 1988 laid down for the first time a national curriculum which all state schools have to teach. It sets out what every child aged from five to 16 should know, understand and be able to do at each stage of their education.

It was introduced because the government felt the gap in academic standards between different schools in different parts of the country was too great. 'In parts it is very good and in others less good, even bad,' said Kenneth Baker, the Conservative education secretary who proposed the changes in the late 1980s.

The aim was to set out an agreed body of knowledge and skills that all children should be taught. National goals of achievement were to be established, against which the progress of all pupils would be measured through regular tests. These standards were considered particularly important for primary schools because too many pupils entered secondary school without the necessary skills in literacy and numeracy, with the result that these children struggled and fell further behind.

What Is the National Curriculum?

The new national curriculum is comprised of 10 subjects (plus Welsh in Wales) and specifies what children should be taught in each of those subjects.

There are three 'core' subjects, so called because they are the most important skills children are expected to master: they are English, mathematics and science.

There are seven 'foundation' subjects: technology, history, geography, a modern language (eg. French, German or Spanish), art, music and physical education. In Wales, schools in Welsh-speaking areas have Welsh as a 'core' subject; for those in English-speaking areas it is a foundation subject.

The 1988 Act also established a system of national tests which children have to take at the ages of seven, 11 and 14, with their results reported to parents.

At the age of 16, children sit the General Certificate of Secondary Education (GCSE), which replaced the old O-levels and CSEs.

Core Subject	Foundation Subject
English	Technology
	History
	Geography
Mathematics	A modern language
	Art
Science	Music
	Physical Education

What Will My Child Study in the National Curriculum?

In primary school, generally attended by children aged five to 11, children have to study nine subjects: English, mathematics, science, technology, history, geography, art, music and physical education.

In secondary school, which most children enter at the age of 11, there are two separate phases to their education.

The first phase spans the ages of 11 to 14: children continue to study the nine subjects they took in primary school and, in addition, they have to study a modern foreign language.

The second phase spans the ages of 14 to 16 and leads to GCSE qualifications. All pupils have to study English, mathematics and science up to the age of 16. They also have to study some technology, a modern foreign language and physical education. They can choose between history and geography or take shorter courses in both. Music and art are optional.

Religious education is compulsory for all children aged five to 16, but it is not part of the national curriculum.

How Does the National Curriculum Work?

The national curriculum affects the way all schools are organised. It marks out distinct phases for each stage of a child's education and establishes common grades for the measurement of pupils' performance.

This section explains how the system works, and the new terms describing the curriculum which are now commonly used in schools.

What Is a Year Group? Phrases such as second form, and fifth form, etc. have largely disappeared from schools. These are now described as 'year groups'. A child generally starts in the 'reception class' of a primary school at the age of four or five. The following year, when most have turned six, they will be in Year One. Most seven-year-olds will be in Year Two, and most eight-year-olds in Year Three. The system continues logically: 11-year-olds are in Year Six, 14-year-olds in Year Nine and 15- or 16-year-olds who are about to take their GCSEs are in Year 11. This terminology is now common to nearly every school, whether grammar, comprehensive or church school.

What Are Key Stages? The national curriculum is divided into four 'key stages' to describe the four phases of a child's education. Pupils reach the end of each key stage around the ages of seven, 11, 14 and 16. The first stage, for pupils aged five to seven, is called Key Stage One (KS1); the second, for pupils aged seven to 11, is Key Stage

Two (KS2); the third, for those aged 11 to 14, is Key Stage Three (KS3); the final stage, for pupils aged 14 to 16, is Key Stage Four (KS4).

Age	Year Group	Key Stages
5	Reception	
6	Year 1	1
7	Year 2	
8	Year 3	
9	Year 4	2
10	Year 5	
11	Year 6	
12	Year 7	
13	Year 8	3
14	Year 9	
15	Year 10	
16	Year 11	4

What Are Attainment Targets? These are the topics within each national curriculum subject, and there are generally four or five for each subject. In English, for example, Attainment Target One is Speaking and Listening. Others include Reading, Writing, Spelling and Handwriting. They are known as 'ATs'.

How Is My Child Tested?

Every child is tested at the end of each key stage when they are seven, 11, 14 and 16. The first part of the testing is carried out by teachers as part of their day-to-day work, where the teacher checks on a child's progress in aspects of the national curriculum. This is an informal approach to testing and is known as teacher assessment.

The second part of the testing comprises formal written tests and specific tasks to assess your child's performance. These are 'SATs', which stands for Standard Assessment Tasks. So, for example, seven-year-olds in summer 1993 had to do basic sums, such as 6p + 1p = ? and 9p - 1p = ?

What Do My Child's Grades Mean?

Your child's performance is measured against a 10-level grading scale. Level 1 sets out the skills, knowledge and understanding expected of a five-year-old of average ability. It is the most basic level.

Children progress from level to level through their school career. The scale is designed so that the average child is expected to move up one level every two years. Therefore, Level 2 defines what is expected of the average seven-year-old, Level 3 the average nine-year-old, Level 4 the average 11-year-old, and Levels 5 to 6 what is expected of the average 14-year-old. Levels 6 to 7 specify what is expected of the average 16-year-old, and further levels up to Level 10 are attainable by the ablest 16-year-olds.

In addition, each subject in the national curriculum has been graded into 10 levels, so a pupil will almost certainly achieve different levels according to ability in each subject. And even within subjects your child may reach different levels in the Attainment Targets for each topic.

The National Curriculum Levels that the Average Child Is Expected to Achieve:

Age	Expected Level
5	One
6	One to Two
7	**Two**
8	Two to Three
9	Three
10	Three to Four
11	**Four**
12	Four to Five
13	Five
14	**Five to Six**
15	Six
16	**Six to Seven**

• the ages in bold are the years in which children sit national tests.

When Will the Curriculum and Tests Be Fully Introduced?

The 10 subjects comprising the national curriculum will not be fully in place for at least another three years. Each subject is being phased in gradually, and English, mathematics and science will be in place for all pupils from September 1993. The last ones – art, music and science – will not be fully in place until 1996.

National tests (SATs) for all seven- and 14-year-olds were scheduled in English, mathematics, science and technology for the summer of 1993, but they collapsed due to boycotts by the teaching unions.

2
What Your Child Will Study at Primary School

The National Curriculum For Children Aged Five to 11

English and mathematics are the most important subjects in primary schools for obvious reasons: a poor grasp of the basic skills of reading, writing and speaking English hampers a child's progress throughout the curriculum, and numeracy or the ability to do simple sums is an essential skill for a child's everyday life. The other subjects are science, technology, history, geography, art, music and physical education.

English

The subject has been divided into three key areas of study:

- Reading

- Writing (including spelling and handwriting)

- Speaking and Listening

These comprise the Attainment Targets (ATs) or topics children have to cover.

Reading

Reading is the most important topic in the English curriculum. It is also an area where you, as a parent, can help significantly by reading with your child either at home or at school.

The curriculum says clearly that teachers should try to encourage parents to participate. In some schools, this will mean that parents are invited into the classroom to read with their children. Most schools allow children to take books home to read with their parents.

A good teacher will regularly spend time listening to your child read on a one-to-one basis, and teachers should introduce their pupils to a wide range of texts, fiction and non-fiction.

Fiction includes nursery rhymes, stories, poems, picture books, folk tales, myths and legends. Examples of the types of books and authors children should read have been drawn up by government advisers, and are listed on pages 82–4.

Non-fiction includes factual books which add to children's knowledge; it also includes everyday written material such as labels, captions, notices, children's newspapers, books of instruction, plans and maps, diagrams, computer print-outs and visual displays.

What Methods Are Used to Teach Reading?

The methods teachers use have been a source of controversy among experts. Most schools use a mixture of methods because different approaches are appropriate for different children.

Reading Schemes: Most schools still use graded reading schemes. These are sets of books specially written to teach children how to read. They are graded according to difficulty and have to be read in the correct sequence. Some of the older schemes have been criticised for being boring, but publishers have improved them in recent years so they are now more imaginative and interesting.

The 'Real Books' Method: This is also known as the 'whole books' approach, and has been criticised in recent years for lacking structure. The thinking behind 'real books' is that children will be more eager to read books that they enjoy, which means using story books which can be bought in a bookshop rather than a structured reading scheme. Few schools adopt this approach exclusively; surveys suggest the figure is as low as one in 20. Indeed, government inspectors have criticised schools that rely solely on a single method. Good schools will undoubtedly have 'real books' which children can take home or read in school, but they will be combined with more structured schemes or approaches for teaching reading.

The Phonic Method: This is a more traditional method of teaching children how to read. Pupils are taught to analyse and build words by sounding letters and combinations of letters. At its simplest, it means saying 'C-A-T says cat', and moves on to more complex words and combinations of letters. Many teachers use it because it gives children the skills they need to decode words when they read, particularly words they may not be familiar with. Critics say the approach can be too mechanical, and that not all words in the English language obey phonic rules.

The Look and Say Method: With this approach children learn to recognise individual words by their shape and pattern. Flashcards with words on them are used in class or even taken home. The cards may have a picture of an object, with the word describing it printed below. As a child's vocabulary increases, he or she learns to make sentences with the cards, and books are used containing the words they have learned. The look and say method is well established in many schools, but children may have problems with words they have not come across before, and those with a weak memory may find it difficult.

Which Is the Most Effective Method? The national curriculum advises schools to use a variety of methods in a balanced way. Relying too much on one approach is certain to leave some children floundering. Some of the most successful schools employ the more traditional phonics method and reading schemes but also use stimulating 'real' story books.

What Makes a School Successful in Teaching Reading?

Government inspectors have identified a number of factors that contribute to success. They include:

- A well-planned reading programme. Good teachers ensure that children use reading schemes as well as a wide variety of fiction, poetry and factual texts.

- A clear reading policy understood by all the staff and explained to parents.

- Regular teaching and practice of phonic skills. This is seen to be of great importance for children aged five to seven.

- Children use books suited to their abilities.

- A good balance between teaching children on a one-to-one basis, in groups, and as a whole class.

- The most successful teachers split children into groups of similar ability for much of the work.

- Pupils are encouraged to concentrate on their tasks and complete them.

- The teachers are keen readers themselves.

- Special events, such as book fairs, book weeks, story-tellers or authors who visit regularly, drama productions and the performance of children's work.

- Formal arrangements for parents to help with reading. This may mean your child will bring home a diary in which you and the teacher comment on and record your child's progress.

You can find out about your school's approach to reading by studying its prospectus. Alternatively, you could speak to the head teacher or your child's class teacher. Schools also hold parents' evenings to discuss such matters.

Findings of government inspectors are contained in *The Teaching and Learning of Reading in Primary Schools 1991*, copies of which can be obtained from Ofsted Publication Centre, PO Box 151, London E15 2HN. (Telephone orders can be made on 081-985-7757: quote publication number HMR 010/91/NS.)

How Can You Help Your Child to Read?

- You will set an example your child can copy if you show an interest in books and reading, whether novels, poetry, newspapers, magazines or any other printed material.

- Are you watching too much television with your child?

- Give books to your baby and read them with him or her. There are many strong cardboard or plastic books that you can buy.

- When you are in or out of the house with your child, point out print wherever it occurs in labels, signs or advertising hoardings, for example. You could turn it into a game.

- Enjoy nursery rhymes and songs with your child. There are also games that you can play such as I Spy, Lotto, Snap or Scrabble. Consult your child's teacher to see what he or she recommends.

- Read with your child regularly, but don't force them to read when they don't want to, or to carry on reading when they are tired. Praise their achievements.

- Provide lots of books for your child to read. All public libraries have good stocks of children's books. Books about their hobbies or interests are a good choice. Better still, take your child with you to the library or bookshops.

- Talk to your child about the stories they have been reading in school during the day.

What Should My Child Be Able to Do?

Each level has a short list of targets that a child has to attain in order to achieve the level. These are known as Statements of Attainment (SoAs) and define the key skills that pupils should acquire.

Most seven-year-olds are expected to achieve Level 2 or above in the national curriculum. Results of the government's classroom tests put 24% of the children at Level 1 or below, 50% at Level 2, 24% at Level 3 and 2% at Level 4. The majority of 11-year-olds should reach Level 4 or above.

Level:	Your child should be able to:	For example:
1 (the average five-year-old)	Recognise that print is used to carry meaning	Point to and recognise their own names
	Begin to recognise individual words or letters	Read simple signs like those on shops. Recognise 'bus stop', 'exit', 'danger' and similar frequent signs
	Talk about stories or information in factual books	Talk about characters and pictures, including their likes and dislikes
2 (the average seven-year-old)	Read accurately and understand straightforward signs, labels and notices	Read labels on drawers in the classroom or simple lists
	Show familiarity with the alphabet	Turn towards the end of a dictionary to find words beginning with s, t and so on
	Use picture and context cues, recognise words on sight and phonic cues in reading	Realise that 'once' is often followed by 'upon a time'
	Describe what has happened in a story and predict what may happen next	Say how and why Jack climbs the beanstalk and what may be at the top
	Listen to a story or poem read aloud and express an opinion about it	Talk about characters, their actions and appearance
	Read a range of material with some fluency, accuracy and understanding	Read something unprompted and talk with confidence about what has been read
3 (the average nine-year-old)	Read aloud expressively and fluently from familiar books	Raise or lower voice to indicate different characters

Level:	Your child should be able to:	For example:
	Listen attentively to stories, talk about setting, story-line and characters and remember important details	Say what happened to change the fortunes of the leading characters in a story
	Show that he or she is starting to use inference and deduction to find meanings beyond the literal context of stories	Discuss what may happen to characters in a story, based on adventures in other stories
	Demonstrate in their writing that they understand how stories are structured	Notice that some stories build up in a predictable way, eg. Goldilocks
	Devise questions to find the information they need in a library	Look up information on, say, the size, colour and habitat of birds for a class project
4 (the average 11-year-old)	Read aloud expressively and fluently with increasing confidence from familiar books	Vary the pace and tone of voice to express feelings, or to represent character or mood
	Explain why they like or dislike stories or poems	Describe the qualities of a story that appeals to them
	Develop the use of inference and deduction in reading stories	Recognise the clues in a text which help a reader to predict events
	Find books in a library by using the classification system, catalogue or database	Use search reading to find information for an inquiry into, say, health and safety at school

For further information or advice, you can contact:

Reading and Language Information Centre, University of Reading, Bulmershe Court, Earley, Reading RG6 1HY. Tel: 0734-318820. (Publishes information, guides and advice on reading)

The Book Trust, Book House, 45 East Hill, London SW18 2QZ. Tel: 081-870-9055. (Publishes lists of books for all ages; please send stamped addressed envelope – SAE)

The Dyslexia Institute, 133 Gresham Road, Staines, Middx TW18 2AJ. Tel: 0784-463935. (Assessment and teaching of children with reading difficulties; send SAE)

The British Dyslexia Association, 98 London Road, Reading RG1 5AU. Tel: 0734-668271. (Advice on children with reading difficulties; send SAE)

What Books Should Your Child Read?

On pages 82–4, there is a list of the types of books and poems which advisers say pupils in primary school should read, but they are not intended to be exclusive. The list provides examples of good quality literature and is intended to be part of a revised English curriculum due to be introduced in September 1994.

Writing

The national curriculum says that children should be taught how to write clear and accurate English, so that they can convey what they mean to other people. They should develop an understanding of different forms of the language and learn how to adapt their writing to suit different purposes and audiences.

The teaching of writing takes many forms. It may be as simple as writing a label for a jar, but it should also include tasks such as composing diaries, stories, letters or accounts of projects completed. Pupils then progress to planning, drafting and revising their written work to develop their ideas and improve presentation.

The aim is to help children not only to write fluently and expressively but to know and understand the basic conventions of English grammar, spelling and punctuation. Good teachers achieve a balance between sensitive correction of children's mistakes in grammar or spelling and allowing them the freedom to express themselves.

The formal and mechanical grammar exercises that were a feature of English lessons in the 1950s have largely disappeared; children are taught about grammar in the course of their writing. However, in recent years there has been a tendency to restore an emphasis on more formal and structured methods of teaching grammar, spelling and punctuation.

Many schools now use word lists, which introduce children to new words they have to learn to spell. They may be families of words with similar phonic sounds, or they may be linked to particular topics or projects pupils are about to study. You as a parent can get involved by helping your child to learn the words.

Good teachers correct children's spelling mistakes, but where a child has particular problems, the teacher may feel that correcting every single spelling mistake will undermine the child's confidence. Standard practice in many schools is for the teacher to spell out a word, let the pupil look at it and then cover it up before the child tries to spell it correctly. Many schools conduct regular spelling tests. Primary school pupils should be taught to use word books and dictionaries to check spellings.

Children of all ages also have to learn how to write on a word processor.

What Your Child Should Be Able To Do

There are three Attainment Targets (ATs), or topics, which cover writing. The first is writing; the second spelling, and the third is handwriting or presentation. The government's tests for seven-year-olds placed 34% at Level 1 or below, 51% at Level 2 and 15% at Level 3.

Level 2 (seven-year-olds)

The seven-year-old of average ability should be able to

- Write a piece of work which has complete sentences. Capital letters and full stops should be used correctly in at least some of the sentences.

- Write a chronological account of an event such as a trip to the park, and compose a story that has a structure, characters and at least one event.

- Spell correctly simple words such as see, car, man, sun, hot, cold, thank.

- Produce legible writing with capital letters, lower case letters and letters such as b, d and p written correctly.

Level 3 (nine-year-olds)

Nine-year-olds of average ability should be able to

- Write a piece of work which has complete sentences, with most full stops and capital letters in the correct places.

- Spell correctly words of more than one syllable such as because, after, open, teacher, animal, together.

- Begin to produce clear joined-up writing.

Level 4 (11-year-olds)

Eleven-year-olds of average ability should be able to

- Write stories which have an opening, a setting, characters, a series of events and an ending.

- Punctuate their work accurately, using paragraphs, capital letters, full stops, question marks, exclamation marks, direct and indirect speech marks and some subordinate clauses.

- Know how to use and spell simple words which begin with prefixes such as un- or in-, and end with suffixes such as -able or -ful.

Speaking and Listening

This topic has been made as much a priority as reading and writing because the ability to communicate clearly and effectively is very important in the modern world.

What Children Learn From Seven To 11

- How to express and justify feelings, opinions and viewpoints with increasing fluency.

- How to assess and interpret arguments and opinions with increasing accuracy and discrimination.

- How to give precise instructions, recount events and narrate stories.

What Your Child Should Know

In the 1992 tests for seven-year-olds, 17% were at Level 1 or below for speaking and listening, 56% at Level 2 and 27% at Level 3. Most 11-year-olds should reach Level 4 or above.

Level 2 (seven-year-olds)

Seven-year-olds of average ability should be able to

- Describe to the teacher or another pupil an event that happened at home or at school.

- Listen attentively to a story or poem, then talk about the characters and what they liked or disliked about it.

- Take part in group activities with other pupils, such as composing a story, designing and making a model or taking a part in a play.

Level 4 (11-year-olds)

11-year-olds average ability should be able to

- Talk in detail about an event or report on, for example, a scientific investigation.

- Ask and answer questions confidently in a variety of situations, such as conducting an interview in a mock radio programme.

- Take part in a group discussion, or draft a piece of writing with other pupils on a word processor.

The Future for English

Significant changes are planned to the English curriculum, which is still only three years old, and these are likely to be introduced in schools from September 1994.

Reading: More emphasis will be placed on phonic methods of teaching children to read.

Writing: This becomes a single Attainment Target, which includes composition, forms of writing, grammar, punctuation, spelling and handwriting, and it is far more precise about what children should know.

Speaking and Listening: The changes require children to be taught standard or grammatically correct English from the age of five.

Mathematics

The teaching of mathematics has changed significantly since the days when primary schoolchildren learned by reciting their multiplication tables. More emphasis is now placed on understanding how to do calculations, how to solve problems and on carrying out practical mathematical investigations. The aim is to make an abstract subject more interesting and appealing to learn. Good schools will make mathematics enjoyable, but they will also use traditional methods whereby children learn tables and learn to add, subtract, multiply and divide by doing sums using pencil and paper.

What Your Child Should Learn and Know

Mathematics is divided into five Attainment Targets (ATs), or topics.

Using and Applying Mathematics: Children learn mathematics in real-life and practical situations, such as how to measure ingredients in cooking.

Number: This includes mental arithmetic. Children learn how to add up, subtract, multiply, divide, estimate and predict.

Algebra: Children as young as five will learn about patterns in sequences of numbers and the use of symbols. By the age of 11, they should have learned about simple formulae and equations.

Shape and Space: This covers basic geometry and some measurement.

Handling Data: Pupils learn how to collect, process and interpret data, ranging from sorting objects to interpreting statistical diagrams.

Children have to learn how to use calculators from their first years in primary school. Clearly, children should also be taught to do mental arithmetic and pencil-and-paper sums without using calculators.

Here are some of the key skills that children should have acquired at seven, nine and 11.

Level 2 (seven-year-olds)

Pupils of average ability should be able to

- Deal with numbers up to 100.

- Add and subtract in their heads, using numbers up to 10. For example, how many pencils will left in a box of 10 if six are removed?

- Work out simple sums involving change when shopping. For example, what is the change from 20p when two biscuits worth 5p and 7p are bought?

- Say what the basic terms of measurement are such as metre, mile, litre, pint, pounds, hour.

- Work out the value of x when $x + 3 = 8$.

- Recognise squares, rectangles, circles, triangles, hexagons, pentagons, cubes, rectangular boxes and cylinders.

Level 3 (nine-year-olds)

Pupils of average ability should be able to

- Deal with numbers up to 1000.

- Do addition and subtraction using numbers up to 20.

- Use multiplication up to 5 x 5 and solve simple sums involving multiplication or division. For example, the cost of four calculators at £2.45 each.

- Do their 2, 5 and 10 times tables.

- Sort two- and three-dimensional shapes, explaining why shapes should be grouped in a particular way.

- Construct and interpret simple bar charts and graphs.

Level 4 (11-year-olds)

Pupils of average ability should be able to

- Do their multiplication tables up to 10 x 10.

- Add and subtract two-digit numbers in their heads, such as 75 – 48.

- Add and subtract two three-digit numbers, without using a calculator, such as 135 + 224 = ?

- Use fractions, decimals or percentages, for example, finding three-tenths of £1, £7 or £10.

- Solve basic algebra problems. For example, if you double a number then add 1, and the result is 49, what is the number?

What Makes a School Successful in Teaching Mathematics?

The gap in achievement between children of the same age is likely to be wider in mathematics than in any other subject, and this means that children in many schools will be grouped according to their ability. A teacher has to ensure that the ablest children are not held back by doing work they find too easy, but equally, the less able should have tasks which challenge them but are not beyond their capacity.

    Mathematics is often taught as a separate, self-contained subject, although children's mathematical skills will be strengthened by work in other areas such as science and technology. School inspectors have identified a number of factors for successful mathematics teaching. They include:

- A mix of approaches so that children are sometimes taught as a whole class, sometimes in small groups and sometimes individually.

- Consistent and constructive marking of work, including a clear analysis of errors and what needs to be done to correct them.

- Work on mental arithmetic including the learning of times tables.

- Well-planned projects which strengthen children's understanding of mathematics, often through work in other subjects such as science and technology.

How Can You Help Your Child with Mathematics?

- Every day there are chances to talk to your child about mathematics. What is the difference, for example, between 'more than' and 'less than', right and left, full and empty, straight and curved?

- Many household activities involve calculations with numbers or sorting shapes, such as arranging the washing, going shopping, weighing ingredients for cooking or measuring a room for shelves.

- Older children can take charge of tasks themselves, such as planning a journey by studying timetables and maps, preparing a meal or simply learning how to budget their pocket money and to buy things.

- There are many games you can play with your child. You could introduce guessing games into conversations; in painting and writing, basic mathematical problems arise about dimensions, angles and numbers. Making models will develop skills of measuring and handling numbers; this could range from making a cardboard box or clothes for a doll to constructing a model kit. There are also dozens of traditional games such as snakes and ladders, ludo, dice or cards based on shapes or numbers.

- There are good mathematical books, puzzles and educational computer software (not just arcade games) that can be bought. Consult your child's teacher on whether there is a particular computer programme or book which could link in with their classwork.

For further information or advice contact:

The Mathematical Association, 259 London Road, Leicester LE2 3BE. Tel: 0533-703877. (Publishes magazines for children)

Society of Young Mathematicians, 5 Tower Road, Orpington, Kent BR6 OSG. Tel: 0689-830380.

Science

The national curriculum was introduced to raise standards, and this is particularly true of science. Before its introduction, some schools taught little or no science, and many children had dropped the subject by the time they reached GCSE. Science is now compulsory for all pupils aged five to 16.

Early primary school science aims to build on children's natural curiosity about the world around them. They should be encouraged to ask questions, to explore and to observe. It is unlikely to involve complex laboratory work; instead, their investigative skills and understanding will be developed through solving problems within their everyday experience.

Teachers will adopt an increasingly systematic approach to teaching science as pupils get older. The national curriculum lays down certain key scientific principles which children should have learned by the time they leave primary school.

What Your Child Should Learn and Know

Science is divided into four Attainment Targets (ATs).

Scientific Investigation: The skills of exploring, investigating, observing, recording and interpreting.

Life and Living Processes: This is the biology element, in which children are taught about plant, animal and human life. It also includes health education. Children aged five to seven learn about the importance of personal hygiene and ways to stay healthy through exercise and what they eat. Among other things, pupils aged seven to 11 are taught about the harmful effects of smoking, alcohol and other drugs.

Materials and Their Properties: The physical and chemical properties of materials, chemical changes, the earth and its atmosphere.

Physical Processes: Electricity, magnetism, energy, forces and their effects, light, sound, the solar system and the universe.

Here are some of the key skills pupils should have acquired in science at the ages of seven and 11:

Level 2 (seven-year-olds)

Pupils of average ability should be able to

- Ask and answer simple scientific questions along the lines of 'how..?' 'why..?' and 'what will happen if..?' For example, why do toy cars go further on a smooth surface than on a rough surface?

- Carry out simple experiments, make observations and draw deductions. For example, mark the distance a car travels along different surfaces and suggest explanations for the differences.

- Know that living things need food, air and water to survive.

- Know that heating or cooling of everyday materials can cause them to melt, solidify or change permanently.

- Know that magnets attract some materials and not others and can repel each other.

- Know that the earth, sun and moon are separate spherical bodies, that light can pass through some materials and how shadows are formed.

Level 4 (11-year-olds)

Pupils of averable ability should be able to

- Prepare and plan an experiment to test a theory. For example, investigate how to keep a container of water hot and whether a thick piece of insulating material will be more effective than a thin piece.

- Name and locate the major organs of the human body and of a flowering plant.

- Place animals and plants in their appropriate groups.

- Understand food chains such as oak tree–caterpillar–blue tit–sparrowhawk.

- Classify materials as solids, liquids and gases, and understand basic chemical changes such as smelting ores into metals.

- Know how measurements of temperature, rainfall, windspeed and direction are used to describe the weather.

- Design and make simple circuits including bulbs, switches and buzzers.

How to Help

A lot of the advice for mathematics applies to science, which is a fundamental part of our everyday lives. Talk with your child about science and encourage their natural questions about the world around them. This will help to improve their skills with language and to develop a curiosity important to scientific inquiry.

- Talk to your child's teacher about ways in which you can help. Some schools allow parents or governors to help as volunteers in class, and there may be specific activities or projects that could be undertaken at home.

- You could involve your children in activities around the house or garden, or take them out on 'expeditions'. It may only be a shopping trip or a walk to the park, but it gives them a chance to explore and learn.

- If your child asks questions you can't answer, have some fun trying to find the answers by looking through books or asking someone who may know.

- Involve your children in your hobbies if they show interest, or they may have their own hobbies. Is there any 'special' trip you could undertake which is related to their hobby?

- Some schools run their own science clubs, and your child is sure to have class projects. There are also national schemes. Ask your school.

For further information, contact:

The Association for Science Education, College Lane, Hatfield, Hertfordshire AL10 9AA. Tel: 0707-267411.

British Association for the Advancement of Science, (British Association of Young Scientists - BAYS), 23 Savile Row, London W1X 1AB. Tel: 071-494-3326.

(Both organisations work closely with teachers to improve links between home and school.)

The Foundation Subjects

There are six other subjects which children must be taught in primary school.

Technology

Technology is compulsory for all children from the ages of five to 16. It may be taught as part of a topic which includes aspects of science and mathematics.

It is a new subject for schools, encompassing the more traditional disciplines of metalwork, woodwork, craft, design and technology (CDT), business studies, home economics and information technology (IT, or computers).

The curriculum aims to teach children how to apply scientific and technical knowledge: this is one of the key areas in which British education falls short. Britain is seen as producing brilliant inventions which are then exploited commercially by our international competitors. Technology is intended to tackle this failing by teaching children how to design, make and evaluate products.

The tasks will get more complex through primary school. They may begin with basic cardboard and glue for constructing a model house. Older children may design and make a model suspension bridge before analysing the advantages of different types of materials.

Technology is divided into five Attainment Targets (ATs) or topics.

Identifying Needs and Opportunities: The needs and potential for design and technology in settings including the home, school, the community, industry and business.

Generating a Design: How to draw up a design proposal to meet the needs they have identified.

Planning and Making: Children are taught how to work out plans to turn designs into products. They should use a wide range of materials, including wood, metal, plastic, clay, textiles and paint.

Evaluating: Learning to assess the advantages or disadvantages of particular materials and designs.

Information Technology: Children as young as five should learn how to work with a computer. By seven, they should be able to store and retrieve information on a computer, and by 11, to use a computer to organise and present work such as a school newsletter. The teaching of word processing skills is included in English, mathematics and science.

History

History is unlikely to be taught as a separate, self-contained subject in the first three years of primary school; it will usually be part of a topic which may include elements of geography, science and English.

Key Stage One: Children aged five to seven will receive a broad introduction to history based largely on their own locality and experiences. This may include visits to local museums and historical sites, and finding out how people lived in the past. They should also learn about historical events.

Key Stage Two: The national curriculum is much more specific about what children should study from seven to 11. It details a minimum of five areas which must be taught. These are:

- Invaders and settlers: Romans, Anglo-Saxons and Vikings in Britain.

- Tudor and Stuart times.

- Victorian Britain and/or Britain since 1930.

- Ancient Greece.

- Exploration and encounters 1450 to 1550 (such as the voyages of Christopher Columbus, Aztec civilisation and the Spanish conquest).

Schools are free to choose when the particular topics are taught during the four years of Key Stage Two. The curriculum also says that children should be taught how to use historical sources such as documents, books and historical sites. The aim is to achieve a balance between knowledge of key facts, and developing investigative skills which make the subject more rewarding and enjoyable.

Geography

This is a subject where you as a parent can play an active part by encouraging your children to study maps or atlases, by watching TV documentaries with them about different parts of the world or the environment, by helping them to study the weather (collecting rainfall, identifying cloud forms, working out symbols on weather forecasts) and making the most of trips (how do we get there, what are the features of the countryside, how is it different to where we live).

Like history, geography is likely to be taught as part of a topic that includes aspects of other subjects. This is particularly so in the early years, when it is very much based on a child's own locality. However, children should also learn the key skills related to geography (how to read a map, measure and observe the weather, and carry out fieldwork) and basic geographical facts including the names and locations of places.

There are five Attainment Targets (ATs) or topics in geography. They are:

Geographical Skills: Much of what is taught will be based on direct experience through field trips, practical activities and exploring their local area.

Knowledge and Understanding of Places: Children from five to seven must study their local area, a different area within the UK and another country. The guidelines are similar for children aged seven to 11 but include a locality in a developing country and one in a European Community country.

Physical Geography: This includes the study of weather, climate, rivers, river basins, seas, oceans, landforms, animals, plants and soils. By seven, pupils should recognise the different forms in which water occurs in the environment such as rain, fog, clouds, ponds, rivers, seas, hail, frost and snow. By eleven, they should be able to identify the different parts of a river, including sources, channel, tributaries and mouth.

Human Geography: This covers the study of population, settlements, communications and economic activities.

Environmental Geography: Environmental issues such as the use and misuse of natural resources, the quality of different environments and the ways they can be protected.

Art, Music and Physical Education

These are the final three subjects which are compulsory for primary school children.

Art: There are two Attainment Targets: Investigating and making, and Knowledge and understanding. All pupils will learn to work in two and three dimensions, use computers where possible and study different types of art from Western and non-Western cultures. Artists suggested for study in primary schools include Henry Moore, Leonardo da Vinci, L.S. Lowry, Vincent Van Gogh, Turner, Constable and Monet.

Music: There are two Attainment Targets: Performing and composing, and Listening and appraising. All pupils should perform a variety of styles of music, use computers to create and record music, and study European classics, British and non-Western music. Composers suggested for study include Tchaikovsky, Mozart, Stravinsky, Bach, Beethoven and Handel.

Physical Education: Children should be able to

swim at least 25 metres by the age of 11 and take part in athletics, dance, games, gymnastics and outdoor pursuits.

These subjects are covered in greater detail in Chapter 8.

Teaching Methods in Primary Schools

There have been dramatic changes in the way that primary school children are taught since the days when pupils sat at desks facing the teacher for lessons such as English, history and geography.

Today, pupils are likely to be seated in groups around a table, studying 'topics' embracing a number of subjects rather than timetabled history or geography.

The movement which prompted these changes believes that children learn best by doing things. It is a shift away from the view of the 1950s that teachers should teach by telling children things.

However, the national curriculum works against the 'topic' approach by identifying specific subjects for study.

Topics or Subjects?

Topic work is most often used for subjects such as science, history and geography, where a common theme means that aspects of each subject can be combined into a single project. For example, one topic might be 'water'.

Many teachers believe that the 'topic' approach has the benefit of allowing projects to be set up for learning through practical experience. However, it is not easy to do well. Government inspectors have commented that at its worst it is 'fragmentary' and 'superficial'. If it is to be successful, it should be well planned, follow the national curriculum closely and focus on a single subject or a few particular subjects.

Teaching the Class as a Whole, in Groups or Individually?

Good teachers will use a mix of methods, teaching children individually, in groups or as a class.

The inspectors feel that many primary teachers do not make enough use of teaching the class as a whole, particularly for history, geography and science. They claim that children can get a lot out of this more 'traditional' approach, where pupils listen to the teacher, are questioned, discuss and receive explanations as a whole class.

When children are divided into groups within the class, some can get less attention because the teacher has to keep moving from one group to another. Where group work is used, the inspectors say teachers should limit the number of activities at any one time in the class to four or less.

Mixed Ability Classes, Mixed Age Classes or Grouping by Ability?

Good teachers set work which matches individual abilities. More able pupils will get more challenging tasks; those less able will get work that is demanding but not beyond them.

One way to do this is to group children according to their abilities and set each group work appropriate to those abilities. This approach, known as banding, setting or grouping by ability, is widely used for mathematics and English.

For some smaller schools, grouping by ability is not possible because there are too few pupils; so children of different ages may have to be taught together. Evidence suggests that work in single age classes is somewhat better than in mixed age classes. The inspectors support the use of grouping by ability, with one important qualification: teachers should not assume that a child's ability is 'fixed', thus preventing a move from a lower group to a higher set.

3
What Your Child Will Study at Secondary School

The National Curriculum for Pupils aged 11 to 16

It is a daunting prospect for a child to start at secondary school, where he or she will be one of the youngest and most junior pupils in a bigger school. Your support could range from simply ensuring that they get to school on time with the proper uniform to encouraging them to talk about their first days.

Most children start secondary school at the age of 11. Some parts of the country have different systems, so that your child may change school at 12, 13 or even 14.

There will be more subjects to choose from, particularly when they reach the ages of 13 or 14 and 16, and there are likely to be different approaches to teaching and to the way the school is organised. There is also more homework, more out-of-school activities and a longer school day.

Key Stage Three

From the ages of 11 to 13 or 14, children continue with the nine subjects they studied at primary school; in addition, they have to do a modern foreign language. These 10 subjects form the basic curriculum (to which religious education is added as the final compulsory part of their studies). Some schools offer additional subjects such as Latin. In Wales, Welsh is a 'core' subject in schools in Welsh-speaking areas and a foundation subject in predominantly English-speaking areas.

Key Stage Four

This is the critical two-year phase when children study for their GCSE examinations. For most pupils, it spans the ages of 14 to 16. They have to continue with English, mathematics and science as well as some study of technology, a foreign language and PE. (In Wales, the status of Welsh is the same as in Key Stage Three.) Pupils also have a choice of other subjects:

Vocational Qualifications: These are now offered by many secondary schools to prepare pupils for a particular kind of job, further training or to supplement more academic courses.

History and/or Geography: Children can choose between history and geography or take shorter courses in both.

Art and/or Music: A pupil can choose whether to continue with music and art, or to drop one or both.

New Subjects: These could include a second foreign language, economics, commerce or classical studies. The choice will depend on the extra subjects your school offers and timetable arrangements. In the year before children start Key Stage Four, the school should discuss with you and your child what options are available.

How Secondary Schools Organise Their Teaching

More Specialised Teaching of Subjects

Your child will have different teachers for different subjects. For many pupils, this is a big change from primary school, where a single class teacher taught the majority of subjects.

Most schools are organised into departments or faculties headed by a senior teacher. These may cover single subjects or groups of subjects. For example, some schools have 'humanities' departments which cover subjects such as history and geography.

Form Teachers and Tutors

Your child will, however, still have a single teacher who effectively acts as a class teacher or tutor. This is organised in different ways. In some schools, the pupils have the same 'tutor' throughout their time at the school; in others, the teacher or tutor is different each year.

Whatever the differences in approach, the aims are the same: to provide your child with someone who is closely involved in his or her welfare, overall academic progress, attendance and behaviour. This is known as the 'pastoral care' system.

House Systems

Many schools have retained house systems as a way of organising pupils. These have traditionally been used for inter-house competitions but they can also fulfil a role in pastoral care, where the housemaster or housemistress and their deputies take responsibility for the general welfare of their pupils.

Other schools have abandoned house systems and base their organisation on year groups with senior teachers in charge of each year.

Setting and Streaming

Secondary schools are more likely to split children into separate teaching groups according to their academic abilities. There are two ways in which this is done. The first is called 'setting', where pupils of similar ability are put in the same teaching group for particular subjects. This may mean that your child is in the top group for mathematics but in the middle group for English or vice versa. The second is called 'streaming', where pupils of similar ability are placed in the same group for all their subjects.

Another term for describing the grouping of children by ability is banding.

Homework

Homework is a part of every secondary school pupil's studies. It is also becoming a more regular feature in primary schools, particularly for older children. Homework is not only an important support for class work but it helps children to work independently.

There are no binding guidelines on how much homework your child should be set, but most schools (and certainly the best) will set it daily. Homework may include writing an essay, reading a set text, gathering information or material for a project or carrying out coursework for GCSE examinations. The amount pupils have to do increases as they progress up the school.

It is an area where parents have an important role to play in taking an interest and in ensuring a quiet place for your child to study.

Good schools provide a homework timetable, so that you know what your child should be doing on a particular day of the week. Most also provide children with homework diaries or personal planners, which you will be asked to monitor and sign every week to ensure work is completed. Some schools run homework clubs for pupils either in the lunch break or after school.

Home–School Contracts

Home–school contracts have been adopted by a number of schools, including some primaries. They are contracts that the school, the child and the parent sign agreeing certain broad principles for each to observe. They may entail ensuring your child completes his or her homework and maintains certain standards of behaviour. It is an initiative that may well extend to many more schools.

Tests and Examinations

Children take the government's national tests in English, mathematics and science at the age of 14. These are likely to be short, written examinations. Their teacher also assesses pupils' performance throughout the year. This involves assessments of their classwork and is likely to include regular written tests set by the teacher. Pupils in Welsh-speaking areas of Wales will have to do national tests in Welsh.

Pupils usually sit GCSE examinations at the age of 15 or 16. In each subject, they will be graded from A at the top to G at the bottom; below that is a U, which stands for ungraded or unclassified. From 1994, the highest mark will be a starred A grade for exceptional achievement which is sometimes described as a Super-A grade.

Children who get an A, B or C at GCSE are judged to have achieved grades equivalent to the old O-level pass. They are still referred to as 'pass' grades by many people, and would be regarded by potential employers as a 'good' pass.

Coursework

Coursework, which students do both at school and at home throughout the year, is an important part of most GCSE examinations. It may be, for example, a written project in English or a practical investigation in science.

The aim is to assess what a student can do apart from a written paper in an examination room, and the marks awarded for the project count towards the final GCSE grade in the particular subject.

The government has imposed certain limits on the amount of coursework that can be included in GCSE courses, but it will account for at least 20% of the student's total marks in most subjects. In technology, the proportion could be as high as 60%.

Careers Education

Pupils should receive specific guidance to help them choose a career. This may include talks by visiting speakers from different professions as well as individual guidance from the school.

It is an area which clearly becomes more important as pupils get older and should certainly have been addressed by their third year at secondary school, when they consider their options for GCSE.

Sex Education

Aspects of sex education are part of the national curriculum for science, including teaching pupils about the HIV virus and Aids. It is up to a school's governors to decide whether to offer sex education beyond that laid down in the curriculum. If they do, they must publish their policy.

Many schools include sex education in personal, social and health education lessons as well as in science and PE. Any sex education provided should encourage pupils to consider moral issues and the value of family life.

New legislation which is due to come into force by September 1994 makes sex education compulsory. Schools no longer have discretion about whether they offer additional lessons in the subject. Parents will, however, have the right to withdraw their children from sex education lessons.

The School Day

The minimum time your child should be taught at each age is laid down in government guidelines.

- For children aged up to seven, it is a minimum of 21 hours of lessons a week.

- For children aged eight to 13, it should be 23.5 hours a week.

- For children aged 14 to 16, it is 25 hours a week – the equivalent of about seven 45-minute periods a day.

Most schools run clubs for pupils after school or during the break. Your school's prospectus or handbook should provide a list of the extra-curricular activities in which pupils can take part.

The National Curriculum Subjects in Secondary Schools

The national curriculum means that all children from the age of 11 to 14 will study a broadly similar syllabus. There will be more variation from the age of 14 to 16 when pupils have more choice.

Some schools allow particularly able pupils to take their GCSE examinations a year early, notably in English and mathematics. This provides time in the following year for them to take more advanced courses in those subjects and/or take GCSEs in additional subjects, such as a second foreign language.

You should be able to look at copies of the national curriculum for each subject at your child's school. Alternatively, they can be obtained from Her Majesty's Stationery Office (HMSO) bookshops. Mail and telephone orders to HMSO, PO Box 276, London SW8 5DT. Tel: 071-873-9090. Fax: 071-873-8200.

English

Nearly all pupils take a GCSE in English. They can also study for an additional GCSE in English literature, but in some schools, this option is restricted to more able pupils. In others, both GCSEs are compulsory.

In the summer of 1994, the GCSE in English will for the first time reflect what is laid out in the national curriculum: the three components are speaking and listening, reading (which includes literature) and writing.

Key Stage Three (Levels 5–6) (what your child should be able to do by the age of 14)

Pupils of average ability will be at Level 5 or 6 in the national curriculum. Here are examples of the things they should be able to do:

- Convey information and ideas effectively, such as providing an eye-witness account of an event.

- Argue for or against a point of view.

- Read a range of fiction and poetry, explaining and justifying preferences.

- Select reference books and use them to find answers to their own questions.

- Tell the difference between fact and opinion in non-fiction texts.

- Write independently reviews, letters, essays, reports, playscripts and stories.

- Spell correctly complex, multi-syllabic words such as medicine, muscular, history and managerial.

Key Stage Four (Levels 6–7) (what your child should be able to do by the age of 16)

Pupils of average ability will be at Level 6 or 7 in the national curriculum. They should be able to

- Adapt language suited to different situations, such as a job interview or an argument with another pupil.

- Express a point of view clearly to a range of audiences.

- Read a range of fiction, poetry, non-fiction and drama, including pre-twentieth century literature.

- Assess the development of a relationship in a play or novel.

- Show a well-developed choice of vocabulary.

- Spell and understand common roots borrowed from other languages, such as micro-(phone), psych-(ologist), tele-(pathy), therm-(ometer) and ch- in Greek words like chaos, chiropody, chorus.

Reading Lists

Your child will almost certainly study works by Shakespeare at secondary school. Government advisers have also drawn up a provisional list of writers for schools, which indicates the types of literature children should study in school.

The list is not definitive, and as a parent you can encourage your child to read widely. However, forcing a child to read a book he or she doesn't want to read can be counterproductive. Set texts which pupils have to study are generally provided by the school.

Pages 82–4 list the books that are part of the revised national curriculum for English, due to be introduced at Key Stage Three from September 1994. It will not be introduced at Key Stage Four until September 1995. The study of at least two plays by Shakespeare is compulsory under the new plans.

Mathematics

Nearly all pupils will take a GCSE in mathematics. More able children may take the examination a year early and go on in the following year to do more advanced courses such as work towards an A/S level in mathematics (the equivalent of half an A-level).

Mathematics is one subject where there will be 'tiered' papers at GCSE, which means that pupils of differing abilities will do papers of varying difficulty. The mathematics teacher will select the papers for which particular pupils should be entered. Some papers will be 'easier', which means that the candidate will be unable to get a grade higher than C, for example.

The five key areas of study (Attainment Targets) in mathematics are using and applying mathematics, number (arithmetic), algebra, shape and space (geometry), and handling data.

As in primary schools, an increasing emphasis has been placed on the application of mathematics: pupils learn to use their knowledge and skills in tasks related to real life.

Key Stage Three (Levels 5–6) (what your child should be able to do by the age of 14)

Pupils of average ability will be at Level 5 or 6 in the national curriculum. Here are examples of the things they should be able to do:

- Calculate mentally 70 x 500 and 800 divided by 20.

- Work out fractions or percentages of quantities such as 1/10th of 2m, 3/5ths of 170m or 15% of £320.

- Understand and use terms such as prime, square, square root, multiple and factor.

- Do pencil and paper calculations such as working out the number of coaches needed to take 167 pupils on an outing when each coach has 42 seats.

- Use accurate measurement and drawing in constructing three-dimensional models.

- Know and use the formulae for finding the areas of squares, rectangles and triangles.

- Solve equations such as $3x + 4 = 10 - x$.

- Plot graphs.

Key Stage Four (Levels 6–7) (what your child should be able to do by the age of 16)

Pupils of average ability will be at Level 6 or 7 in the national curriculum. Here are examples of the things they should be able to do:

- Calculate with fractions, decimals, percentages or ratios, and use estimates to check calculations.

- Solve equations such as $x^2 = 5$, and $2x - y = 9$, $x + 3y = 8$

- Know and use formulae for finding the areas and circumferences of circles.

- Multiply and divide mentally single-digit multiples of any power of 10, such as working out 80 x 0.2 and 600 divided by 0.2.

- Use a calculator effectively to solve problems such as converting inches to centimetres, given that 0.394 inches = one centimetre.

- Use Pythagoras' Theorem and use co-ordinates (x, y, z) to locate positions in three dimensions.

Science

Schools have different ways of organising their science curriculum. Some still teach physics, chemistry and biology as separate and distinct subjects. Others have amalgamated the three into one subject called 'balanced science'.

Pupils taking 'balanced science' will still cover physics, chemistry and biology. It was introduced because too many children were dropping one or more of the individual sciences simply because there was not enough time to cover them all.

If a school offers balanced science, your child will probably have to decide, in the year before they start their GCSE courses, whether to do a single or double award in the subject at GCSE.

Both single and double science cover the three sciences (physics, chemistry and biology), but one is narrower than the other.

Double Science is more comprehensive and is the equivalent of two GCSEs. Inevitably, it will take more time, probably at least 20% of the timetable, and is likely to fill a two-subject slot on school timetables.

Single Science is less comprehensive and therefore takes less time. An inquiry by government inspectors concluded that single science was inadequate preparation for those who might want to go on and do science A-levels.

Separate Sciences: Science taught as three separate subjects will account for up to one-third of pupils' lesson time. If this is the model adopted by your child's school, he or she cannot drop out of any of them and has to take all three through to GCSE examination.

You should have the chance to discuss the options with your child's school. It is important to give careful consideration to the choices in science because opting for single science may limit options at A-level and subsequent choices of career.

The national curriculum has been designed to reinforce the move towards balanced science. There are four broad areas of study (or Attainment Targets):

- Scientific investigation (developing skills of investigation, observation and interpretation)

- Life and living processes (biology)

- Materials and their properties (chemistry)

- Physical processes (physics)

Key Stage Three (Levels 5–6) (what your child should be able to do by the age of 14)

Pupils of average ability will be at Level 5 or 6 in the national curriculum. Here are examples of the things they should be able to do:

- Name the major organs (and their functions) in mammals and flowering plants.

- Classify aqueous solutions as acidic, alkaline or neutral, using indicators.

- Know how switches, relays, variable resistors, sensors and logic gates can be used to solve simple problems.

- Draw diagrams showing orbits of the planets in the solar system and indicate how long it takes each to complete its orbit.

Key Stage Four (Levels 6–7) (what your child should be able to do by the age of 16)

Pupils of average ability will be at Level 6 or 7 in the national curriculum. Here are examples of the things they should be able to do:

- Know the ways in which animals and plants have adapted their size, shape and behaviour to their natural environment in order to survive.

- Explain the physical differences between solids, liquids and gases in simple particle terms.

- Understand the qualitative relationships between current, voltage and resistance.

- Know where the solar system is in the Milky Way galaxy.

Modern Foreign Languages

Pupils have to study a foreign language from the age of 11 to 16. However, in Key Stage Four pupils aged 14 to 16 may have the option of doing a shorter course in a foreign language combined with another subject.

Schools can choose which languages to teach from a list of 19, but what they can offer will depend on the expertise and number of teachers. The working group of experts who drew up the guidelines warned of difficulties in introducing the curriculum in foreign languages because of a shortage of trained teachers.

By law, schools have to offer at least one European Community language. For the vast majority, this will be French. The next most popular is German, followed by Spanish. Many offer pupils the option of a second foreign language even though this is not obligatory. The full list of 19 languages is:

European	Non-European
Danish	Arabic
Dutch	Bengali
French	Chinese (Cantonese or Mandarin)
German	
Greek	Gujarati
Italian	Hebrew
Portuguese	Hindi
Spanish	Japanese
	Panjabi
	Russian
	Turkish
	Urdu

Language teaching has changed significantly over the past two decades, and there is now more emphasis on how to speak the language rather than the traditional drilling in verbs and grammar. This means that pupils learn the language in more realistic situations such as writing to foreign pen-pals or watching foreign TV programmes, and perhaps reading and performing plays.

The new national curriculum for modern languages was introduced in September 1992 in secondary schools and it applied only to 11-year-old pupils starting Key Stage Three. It will not be introduced for 14-year-olds at Key Stage Four until September 1995.

The curriculum is divided into four main areas of study, or Attainment Targets. They are:

- Listening (understanding spoken language)

- Speaking (expressing oneself effectively in speech and conversation)

- Reading (understanding and responding to written language)

- Writing (conveying meaning in written language)

What Your Child Should Be Able to Do

At age 11 to 12

The pupil of average ability should be able to

- Respond to basic questions and commands such as 'Shut the door'.

- Say such words as cat and house when shown a photo.

- Copy words and familiar phrases, write a shopping list, write several sentences.

At age 14

The pupil of average ability should be able to

- After a video, discuss the subjects' jobs, follow map directions, take details from the telephone and identify from an announcement what is being said.

- Offer an explanation as to why something happened, sustain some conversation, put words in the correct order and use the correct forms of address such as *'tu'* and *'vous'*.

- Respond to a written inquiry, identify facts in a newspaper article, reply to a letter.

At age 16

The average child should be able to

- Listen to a radio report and make notes, listen to a talk and list the arguments, identify the main points of a television interview.

- Converse intelligibly in a foreign language.

- Understand selected writings from newspapers, magazines or advertisements.

- Write to a new penfriend about a recent family holiday.

Technology

Technology is a new subject in the national curriculum and has to be studied by all pupils aged 11 to 16.

Many schools will offer the option of doing a 'short' course in technology from the age of 14 to 16 (Key Stage Four), but this has to be combined with another subject to lead to a GCSE qualification. Nearly thirty combinations are offered by the examining boards, including technology and art, technology and economics, and technology and business studies. Your child's school is likely to offer only some of these combinations.

Pupils who decide on a short course in technology must include an element of information technology in their studies to develop their skills in using computers. There is also a GCSE in Information Systems, which replaces the old subject of Computer Studies.

The new technology curriculum was only introduced for younger secondary school pupils in 1990, and is being introduced for older pupils at Key Stage Four from September 1993.

This is proving difficult for some schools because of shortages of equipment and of staff with the necessary expertise, and is further complicated by changes being made to the technology curriculum.

Technology covers the traditional disciplines of metalwork, woodwork, craft, design and technology (CDT), business studies, home economics and information technology. It is divided into five main areas of study (Attainment Targets). The aim is to teach pupils how to identify the need for a particular product, draw up a design to meet that need, then plan and make the product, so as to evaluate whether it is effective and successful.

The five areas are: identifying needs and opportunities; generating a design; planning and making; evaluating; information technology.

Levels 5–6 (what your child should be able to do by the age of 14)

- Draw up a plan for an automatic greenhouse watering system.

- Take account of factors (such as the length of time paint takes to dry) in devising a plan for a product.

- Be able to justify why particular materials were used.

- Edit a newspaper for parents, using a computer.

Levels 6–7 (what your child should be able to do by the age of 16)

- Show how to evaluate a prototype product through experiments, tests or pilot models. Modify the product in light of the results.

- Produce a design specification for toddlers' clothing, for example, and choose materials that meet the specification.

- Design and make a piece of jewellery taking account of the different properties of the materials (eg. soft versus hard metals).

- Use a desk-top publishing program to join text, images and graphs in a report on a scientific experiment.

The Other Foundation Subjects

History and Geography are compulsory for all pupils aged 11 to 14. The national curriculum for the two subjects was introduced for younger secondary school children in 1991, but will not be introduced for pupils aged 14 to 16 (Key Stage Four) until September 1994.

The government proposes that pupils should not be allowed to drop both subjects at the age of 14; they will have a choice of studying either, or short courses in both. The form of the short courses has yet to be decided.

Music and art are compulsory until 14, when pupils have the option to drop one or both. Physical education is obligatory from 11 to 16, although study at Key Stage Four is less comprehensive unless children are taking a GCSE in the subject.

See Chapter 8 for more details on the music, art and PE curriculum.

History

History is divided into three broad topics aimed at teaching not only historical facts but how to make use of original material such as documents, books, pictures and historical sites. The three Attainment Targets are: knowledge and understanding of history; interpretations of history; use of historical sources.

Key Stage Three

For children aged 11 to 14, the following periods are compulsory:

- The Roman Empire.

- Medieval Britain 1066 to 1500.

- The making of the United Kingdom: crowns, parliaments and peoples 1500 to 1750.

- Expansion, trade and industry: Britain 1750–1900.

- The Second World War.

Pupils have a choice of other topics where they do more detailed studies.

Key Stage Four

For children aged 14 to 16, the following periods are compulsory.

- The development of British democracy 1900–1960s, including the extension of the right to vote and the formation of the welfare state.

- International conflict and co-operation 1945–1960s, including superpower relations since the Second World War, the break-up of the European empires and the United Nations.

- Economic, social and cultural change in the twentieth century.

Pupils who do a full GCSE have also to study a theme in British history from 1500 to the present day and a country or region other than Britain in the twentieth century.

Geography

Geography is divided into five topics. At Key Stage Three, pupils aged 11 to 14 will study:

- Geographical skills (including drawing, reading and interpreting maps, land measuring and recording the weather).

- Knowledge of places (including their local area, a region, a European Community country and one economically developing country).

- Physical geography (including studies of river systems, earthquakes, volcanoes, erosion, climate and soil).

- Human geography (including population studies, transport systems, town planning, land use and economic development).

- Environmental geography (including mining, energy sources, planning and management of the environment).

Pupils who study geography at Key Stage Four follow the same topics, but in more depth. For example, their study of places will include a more comprehensive analysis of one country in the EC selected from France, Germany, Italy or Spain. They will have to look in detail at one economically developing country from Bangladesh, Brazil, China, Egypt, Ghana, India, Kenya, Mexico, Nigeria, Pakistan, Peru or Venezuela. They must also undertake a comparative study of the USA, Japan and Russia, then choose one on which to do a more detailed project.

How Can You Help Your Child at Secondary School?

Here are some suggestions for supporting your child at secondary school.

Helping with Homework: Try to ensure that your child has a well-lit place to do homework without distractions, and that they have the necessary equipment such as notebooks, pencils and pens. If children learn to study on their own at an early age, they are unlikely to lose the habit. It becomes harder to develop the skill when they are older.

Work out a structure to the evenings so that there is a specific time when they do their homework – perhaps set times before or after the evening meal. Snatched moments of work are never satisfactory.

You can help with basic skills and learning exercises such as spelling, multiplication or new foreign words.

Show an interest in their work at home or at school. Spare time to listen to their problems or simply to talk to them about their day at school.

Many schools have homework diaries which you should complete to ensure they are doing their work. Schools also provide homework timetables so that you can check what work should be done on particular days. Check that homework has been marked.

If your children have difficulties with their homework, be prepared to help and guide them but do not do the work for them. If it is clearly too hard or too easy, you should speak to their teacher. If you feel your child is not getting enough homework, again, speak to his or her tutor or teacher. It may be that your child is not doing what has been set or has indeed not been set enough.

Similar Principles Apply to Coursework. You may be able to help with your child's research for a project. This does not mean that you do it but you could guide your child to where information could be found. You may even be a source of information yourself if, for example, the project is connected with your work or one of your hobbies.

Supporting Your Child During Examinations and Tests: Revising for examinations can be a stressful time for children. 'Parents should be seen and not heard at examination revision time,' says George Turnbull, of the Associated Examining Board. 'They can offer encouragement, care, attention, tea and sympathy but they musn't nag.'

Turnbull's examination guide for pupils, *How to Do Better in Exams*, can be obtained free of charge from Barclays Bank Information Centre, PO Box 63, Coventry CV4 8JU. It emphasises the importance for pupils of planning their revision and preparing for examinations.

Buying or Borrowing Text Books: Schools will provide set course books but because of limited resources this is not an easy task for many schools. If you wish to buy text books for your child, you should consult the school, because it is pointless buying a text book unrelated to your child's work. There may be local libraries you could visit with your child to get the books he or she needs.

Attending Parents' Evenings: Schools hold regular parents' evenings where you can discuss your child's progress with his or her teachers and find out what they will be studying in the coming term or year. They are important.

Reading School Reports: Many schools now have sections within school reports where you can write your comments alongside your child's and the teacher's. It hardly needs to be said that school reports are one of the most important sources of information about your child's progress.

Involvement with the School: Nearly all schools have parents' and/or parent–teacher associations, which you can join. Parents are also being encouraged to join governing bodies of schools.

Private Tuition: This is an option for those who can afford it. It is also an issue that needs to be tackled sensitively. Even the best schools may see private tuition as an implicit criticism of their teaching.

It may be worth consulting your school to ensure that any extra tuition complements class work. Some schools do provide additional courses, help or specialist clubs for pupils. These may involve work to extend their knowledge and skills or specific support for those who may be struggling.

Helping with, or Organising, Out-of-School Activities: Many schools run extra-curricular activities and clubs. They may coincide with an interest or hobby of your own and in which your expertise could be helpful, or you may be able to encourage and support your child's interests.

There are also a growing number of out-of-school weekend and summer courses geared towards particular subjects in the national curriculum, ranging from mathematics and science to foreign languages.

4

Choices at 14 and Beyond

Choices for 14-Year-Olds

The third year in secondary school (Year Nine) is the time when pupils have to decide their options for the critical last two years of their compulsory education (Key Stage Four).

The choice of subjects is particularly important because it will have significant bearing on what pupils will be able to do when they complete their GCSE studies at the age of 16. Opportunities for certain careers, training or A-levels can be limited if particular subjects are dropped at the age of 13 or 14. Careers advisers stress, therefore, that it is important for pupils to keep their options open when they make decisions at this time. This generally means that children should choose as wide a range of subjects as possible.

Certain subjects are compulsory. They are English, mathematics, science, technology, a modern language, history and/or geography and PE. Most pupils will take GCSEs in the core subjects of English, mathematics and science. Only those who are judged to be at Level 3 or below will not have to sit GCSE examinations in these subjects.

There are a host of other subjects from which pupils can choose, although the range of choice will depend on a school's resources, the demand for those subjects and timetable arrangements. Some, such as sociology or economics, will be new. There will also be an increasing number of 'short courses', where pupils can combine subjects to get a single GCSE.

Schools will detail the range of courses and subjects for Key Stage Four in their prospectuses or in separate pamphlets.

What Children Have to Study from 14 to 16

English	Full GCSE course
Mathematics	Full GCSE course
Science	Single certificate science, double certificate science or separate sciences
Welsh	Full GCSE course or a short course combined with another subject. Pupils taught in Welsh-speaking schools have to take a full GCSE course in Welsh. Those in English-speaking schools have the option of a short course
Technology	Full GCSE course or a short course combined with another subject
Modern Languages	Full GCSE course or short course combined with another subject
Geography/History	Full GCSE course in one or both, or short course in both
Physical Education	Compulsory. Pupils not taking a GCSE in PE, dance or any other related activity have to study at least two of the following: athletics, dance, games, gymnastics and outdoor activities
Religious Education	Compulsory. Children have to do religious education but do not have to take a GCSE in the subject

Vocational Qualifications

These have been introduced in many schools as additional options for pupils aged 14 to 16 to help prepare them for the world of work. Many provide specific skills for a particular type of job, career or further training after pupils leave school. Most lead to qualifications or certificates.

They can be taken as a supplement to more academic subjects or as a foundation for and introduction to the larger number of vocational qualifications available at 16. They range from practical qualifications, such as certificates for typing, to more general courses covering subjects such as administration, production and business.

The government is keen to increase vocational courses for this age group and to change some perceptions that they are second best to GCSE and A-level qualifications. A new qualification is being introduced in schools and colleges, called the General National Vocational Qualification (GNVQ). It is primarily being offered to students over 16.

Many schools are also part of the Technical and Vocational Education Initiative (TVEI), a national government-funded project designed to develop skills in 14 to 18 year-olds which will help them in the world of work. Individual schools' approaches to TVEI will be different, though all will include work experience, careers advice, personal counselling and emphasis on technological qualifications.

Choices for 16-Year-Olds

There are broadly four options for students who have completed their GCSE studies. They can:

- Continue with their academic studies (A-levels and/or GCSEs)

- Opt for a vocational/job-related course

- Go on to a youth training scheme

- Seek a job

Much will depend on their GCSE results, which are released in August, and any other qualifications they have gained at school.

In deciding which route to take, it is worth taking advice from the school, teachers and your local authority careers advisory service.

Compulsory schooling ends at 16, so all pupils are free to leave and enter youth training or seek a job, whatever their qualifications. However, if they have at least four GCSEs at grades A to C, they may be able to do A-levels. Alternatively, they could do a vocational course. If they have a few GCSEs, or even no GCSEs, there is still the option of a vocational course and/or taking more GCSEs.

School or College?

Sixteen-year-olds who want to add to their qualifications can choose where they want to go. They can stay on in the sixth form at their present school to take A-levels or re-take GCSEs. A growing number of schools also offer vocational courses in the sixth form.

There will be some areas of the country where schools will not have their own sixth form. There will, however, be a local sixth form college, a sixth form centre or a tertiary college where they can continue their academic studies. An increasing number of these also provide vocational courses. Even if a student's school has a sixth form, he or she still has the option of leaving to continue academic studies elsewhere. This is essentially a personal choice.

A sixth form college may have a wider choice of subjects, everyone is of a similar age and it possibly offers a more adult environment. Alternatively, staying at the same school with familiar surroundings and teachers may be a more attractive option.

The third choice is to go to a college of further education (FE), which also offers A-level courses. Traditionally, FE colleges have provided a wider range of vocational courses, and have a broader mix of students, attending full-time and part-time courses.

More GCSEs

Pupils aged 16 have the option of re-taking GCSEs to improve their grades, or studying for new subjects with some re-takes. It is important to seek advice from the school about whether this would be a sensible decision. Fewer than half the students who spend a year taking GCSEs in the sixth form end up with four or more at grades A to C.

A-Levels

A-levels are two-year courses offered in most subjects, and are usually taken by students seeking to go on to higher education.

It is important that pupils discuss their choice of A-levels with teachers, who can give clear guidance on what will be expected of them during the two years. They will know the pupil's strengths and should be able to advise on suitable subjects to take.

If your child's ambition is to go on to higher education, it is important to check university requirements for particular subjects. They may want particular GCSEs and A-levels, and teachers can be consulted on this. The information is also contained in *University and College Entrance, The Official Guide*, stocked by most libraries, schools, local careers service offices and many bookshops.

Competition for university places is fierce in many subjects, particularly in the arts and social sciences where high A-level grades are required for many courses, and this should be borne in mind when choosing subjects. Given that teachers deal with the universities every year, they are best placed to give advice on such issues. Career opportunities should also be taken into account.

More than 60 subjects are offered at A-level. School and college prospectuses should detail which A-levels are on offer.

Students will normally take two or three A-levels in broadly similar groupings, such as arts or sciences.

A/S levels can also be taken at many schools. These are two-year courses, which cover about half the syllabus of a full A-level but are just as difficult. They are designed to give students a broader choice and education so that a candidate doing a science-based group of A-levels could, for example, take an A/S level in an arts subject.

Vocational Qualifications

Vocational courses have traditionally been provided by further education colleges, but more schools are now offering them as an alternative to the purely academic route of A-levels. This is a move supported by employers.

More universities are also prepared to take candidates with vocational qualifications. More than one in 10 students now on degree courses won their places on this basis.

The improved status of vocational courses has been endorsed by the government, which is introducing a new national system of qualifications for schools and colleges called General National Vocational Qualifications (GNVQs). GNVQs and NVQs will become the common currency for vocational qualifications, replacing the confusing array of different qualifications offered in the past by different groups. GNVQs are designed to prepare students over 16 for a range of related occupations as well as for higher education. They are divided into five levels, representing different degrees of competence. The table on page 35 explains how each is broadly equivalent to other academic qualifications and the type of job they might lead to.

The National Council for Vocational Qualifications, which is overseeing the changes, has accredited three awarding bodies to offer GNVQs: the Business & Technology Education Council (BTEC), City and Guilds (C&G) and the RSA Examinations Board.

About 1000 schools and colleges will be offering GNVQs from September 1993 in art and design, business, health and social care, leisure and tourism, and manufacturing. Other subjects will follow in subsequent years.

The intention is that one in four 16-year-olds will be taking GNVQs by 1996, when it is hoped that GNVQs in at least two subjects will be available in more than 1500 schools. The eventual aim is for half of the country's 16- and 17-year-olds to be studying for them, but the change-over will take time, so it is useful to understand the present range of awards. The three main bodies who have traditionally provided vocational qualifications are BTEC, C&G and the RSA Examinations Board.

Business & Technology Education Council (BTEC) offers awards in a wide variety of subjects including business, engineering and construction. They are available at three levels.

- BTEC First: Around GNVQ intermediate level. It is normally taken by school-leavers or sixth-formers who have chosen the general area of work they wish to enter, and generally requires one year of study.

- BTEC National: GNVQ advanced level. The normal entry requirement is four GCSEs at grades A to C or a BTEC first. It generally requires two years of study, and is increasingly available in schools and colleges. Can lead on to employment or to higher education.

- BTEC Higher National: Around GNVQ level four. It usually requires two years of study, and the normal minimum entry requirement is one A-level or a BTEC National. It is generally

GNVQ Level	Description	Equivalent
Foundation (Level 1)	One-year basic vocational course	4 GCSEs at grades D to G
Intermediate (Level 2)	Basic technician course	4+ GCSEs at grades A to C
Advanced (Level 3)	Technician, Advanced craft, Supervisor	2+ A-levels
4	Higher technician, Junior management	Higher education
5	Profession, Middle management	Postgraduate

available in colleges of further education and of higher education, and many universities.

City and Guilds (C&G) also offers a range of awards which are popular with schools and colleges in areas such as engineering, construction, catering, hairdressing and community care. As with BTEC, there is a range of levels. One of their most popular qualifications is the Diploma of Vocational Education (which is replacing the Certificate of Pre-Vocational Education – CPVE). This is designed primarily for students who may not have a clear idea of the job they want to do but want to learn skills relevant to the world of work.

The three levels are:

- Foundation level, for students aged 14 to 16. They work on case studies in at least one of six broad vocational areas. That work can go towards GCSE assessment. It includes some time on work experience.

- Intermediate level is for students over 16; it can be studied over two years alongside A-levels or on its own in one year. Students can choose from more than 100 'modules' (units of study) in nine vocational areas, and may have the chance to be credited with a GNVQ at level two.

- National level is a two-year programme of study for students aged over 16, which is to be aligned with GNVQ level three.

RSA Qualifications have been widely available in schools and colleges for many years. RSA also offers GCSEs which focus on developing skills relevant to jobs. Some RSA courses develop single skills useful at all levels, such as word processing and information technology, which may take only a few weeks of study. Other qualifications cover a full range of levels.

Youth Training

Any student of 16 or 17 who has left school or college and is unemployed is guaranteed a place on a youth training programme, if he or she wants it. It generally involves on-the-job training, sometimes with a part-time college course.

Youth training is provided by local employers, colleges, training companies, local authorities or voluntary organisations, and information can be obtained from your local authority careers service. Young people under 17 who take up this option receive a minimum allowance of £29.50, rising to £35 from their seventeenth birthday (1993 figures). Most of those who complete their training go into jobs or further education, and half of those finishing their training gain a qualification.

Some areas have introduced a scheme of training credits. These are issued to school-leavers by Training and Enterprise Councils (local groups of employers), who are now responsible for the youth training programme. The credits can be used to 'buy' training from an employer or college. The training may involve day or block release courses, evening classes or home study packages.

Getting a Job

The final option is to try to find a job. School-leavers should consider whether the jobs also include training. The local careers service and job centre will be your main points of contact. More 16-year-olds than ever before are deciding on further training or education.

What Do Most People Do?

About two-thirds (65%) of 16-year-olds stay on in education to get further qualifications. Some 13% go on to youth training. One in 12 (7.8%) get jobs, according to figures from local authority careers services in 1992. The remainder are unemployed, or their situation is unknown.

Further Information

Useful Addresses

National Council for Vocational Qualifications, 222 Euston Road, London NW1 2BZ. Tel: 071-387-9898.

Business and Technology Education Council, Central House, Upper Woburn Place, London WC1H 0HH. Tel: 071-413-8400.

City and Guilds, 326 City Road, London EC1V 2PT. Tel: 071-278-2468.

RSA Examinations Board, Westwood Way, Coventry CV4 8HS. Tel: 0203-470033.

School Examinations and Assessment Council (SEAC), Newcombe House, 45 Notting Hill Gate, London W11 3JB. Tel: 071-229-1234. (Oversees national tests, GCSE and A-level)

National Curriculum Council (NCC), Albion Wharf, 25 Skeldergate, York YO1 2XL. Tel: 0904-622533. (Oversees the national curriculum)

School Curriculum and Assessment Authority (SCAA), Newcombe House, 45 Notting Hill Gate, London W11 3JB. Tel: 071-229-1234. This new authority will be created from 1 October 1993, from the merger of NCC and SEAC. It will replace NCC and SEAC.

Useful Reference Books

Pupils should ask careers advisers to help them find some of the following books or pamphlets, most of which should be in school, in careers offices or in local libraries.

Which Subject? Which Career? A guide by the Careers Research and Advisory Centre (CRAC). Available by post or phone from Biblios, PDS Ltd, Star Road, Partridge Green, West Sussex RH13 8LD (tel: 0403-710971), or the Consumers' Association bookshop, 359–361 Euston Road, London NW1. Tel: 071-486-5544.

Decisions 13/14+; Decisions 15/16+; Your Choice of A-levels. Three guides by CRAC, published by Hobsons Publishing. Available by post or phone from Biblios, PDS Ltd, Star Road, Partridge Green, West Sussex, RH13 8LD. Tel: 0403-710971.

Occupations '94; Working In Booklets. Two guides published by COIC, PO Box 348, Bristol, BS99 7FE. Tel: 0272-777199.

It's Your Choice, also published by COIC, available free of charge and generally distributed to all 15-year-olds in school.

Databases

Three computerised information services give full details of courses. They are available in many careers offices and some schools.

EECTIS – Educational Counselling and Credit Transfer Information Service

TAP – Training Access Point

National Database of Vocational Qualifications

5
Tests and Examinations

The national curriculum established a framework for testing all pupils. The aim is to give parents information on their child's progress at school, to help teachers identify the strengths and weaknesses of each pupil and to provide results that enable the effectiveness of individual schools to be measured.

Methods of Testing at Seven, 11 and 14

The progress of children is measured by teachers through a combination of teacher assessment and national tests.

Teacher Assessment is a more informal method of measuring progress. It is carried out by the teacher during the course of a child's classroom exercises and work. These assessments form the basis for annual school reports to parents.

National Tests at the ages of seven, 11 and 14 are taken by all children in English, mathematics and science. They are more formal tests, often involving short written exercises that have to be completed within a set time. They are frequently described as Standard Assessment Tasks, or SATs. All children sit them during the spring or summer term.

Other Internal Tests continue to be used by many schools. These may be tests that they have developed themselves, used for years and still find helpful. There are also a number of commercial tests that some schools and local education authorities still use to measure children's reading abilities. These determine whether a child is reading at a standard appropriate to their age.

Tiered Test Papers are used even at the age of seven. This means that children of differing abilities will sit different papers in which they will only be able to get a certain range of grades. For example, there were four mathematics papers that 14-year-olds could take in 1993. The first covered Levels 1 to 4, the second Levels 3 to 6, the third Levels 5 to 8 and the fourth Levels 7 to 10. The less able sat the first paper and the brightest took the fourth paper. The differences in achievement are wider among older pupils. Tiered papers are therefore more likely to be used at the top end of primary school and in secondary schools.

Methods of Testing at 15 or 16

GCSEs are national examinations that are taken by nearly all children at the ages of 15 or 16. GCSE is an acronym for the General Certificate of Secondary Education. It largely involves written examinations that pupils sit during the summer term.

Coursework is an element of most GCSEs. Candidates have to complete the work during the two years before they sit their examinations. It may, for example, involve practical projects that are then written up. It is designed to assess children's abilities outside the pressured atmosphere of an examination room.

Reporting the Results to Parents

At least once a year parents should receive a school report on their child's progress. It must include details of the child's progress in all the national curriculum subjects as well as in any additional subjects or activities. There will also be information on the child's attendance and general progress, and on arrangements for parents to discuss the report with the school. At the ages of seven, 11 and 14, parents must also be told their child's results in the national tests in English, mathematics and science. This will include information about the levels the child achieved in each of the main topics within each of the subjects. At the age of 16, parents should get a report giving the grades awarded to their child in each of their GCSEs and any other qualifications.

For parents of A-level students, the report should give the subjects their child entered, grades achieved and points score. (See page 59 for an explanation of A-level points scores.)

National Tests at Seven, 11 and 14

The national tests for 1994 and subsequent years have been changed by the government following the concerns expressed by teachers. Children aged seven will sit compulsory national tests in English, mathematics and science. Pupils aged 14 will also take compulsory tests in the same subjects. There will be national pilots of tests for pupils aged 11, which means that it will be left up to the school to decide whether to administer them.

Tests for Seven-Year-Olds

The tests are taken at the end of Key Stage One, during the spring and/or summer term of Year Two. Many of the children in the class are likely to be seven and in their third year at primary school.

The tests focus on the basics of reading,

writing, arithmetic, spelling and scientific knowledge. Chapter 2 will give you some idea of the standards expected of your child.

What Do the Grades Mean?

Pupils will attain one of four levels in each of the 'core' subjects of English, mathematics and science. They will also be given a level for each of the main topics within those subjects.

The results from the tests, which were introduced nationally in 1991, show that a small percentage of children will not yet be at Level 1. In broad terms, Level 1 is below what is expected of a seven-year-old of average ability, Level 2 is average, Level 3 is above average and Level 4 is exceptional. Your child is likely to achieve different levels in different subjects and even in the different topics within those subjects.

The table for 1992's test results shows the proportion of children nationally at each level in each of the subjects. It must be emphasised that these are national figures. There are wide differences in results for different areas of the country.

What Will the Tests Involve?

The exact form and style of the tests for 1994 has yet to be decided. However, they will cover some of the targets in the national curriculum. Examples from 1993 tests will give you a broad idea of the types of questions.

National Tests For Seven-Year-Olds (1992)

Subject	% Level 1	% Level 2	% Level 3	% Level 4
English	22	56	21	0
Reading	23	50	24	2
Writing	32	51	15	0
Speaking and Listening	15	56	27	0
Spelling	21	57	19	1
Mathematics	20	69	9	0
Arithmetic	33	48	15	0
Number, Algebra and Measures	20	69	9	0
Science	11	68	20	0

English

Pupils judged to be at Level 2 or above had to read a short book (*The Greedy Fox and other stories* by Aesop) and answer questions on it. They were then graded.

There were also compulsory spelling tests for pupils at Level 2 or above. Children had to fill in the following words in their copy of a story read out by the teacher. Words for Level 2 included: his, out, met, keep, turn, sing, edge, fly, hurry, anything, saw, blue, across, beside, beautiful, full.

Words for Level 3 included: underground, forest, everything, uninteresting, furniture, holiday, journey, certainly, astonished, noises, several, suddenly, straight, arrived, misfortunes, thought, although, perhaps.

Who came to speak to the fox?

English Level 2 (1993)

1 2 3 4

Mathematics

Here and opposite are some of the questions that children had to answer to achieve particular levels. The two questions on this page are at Levels 1 and 2 from the 1993 tests.

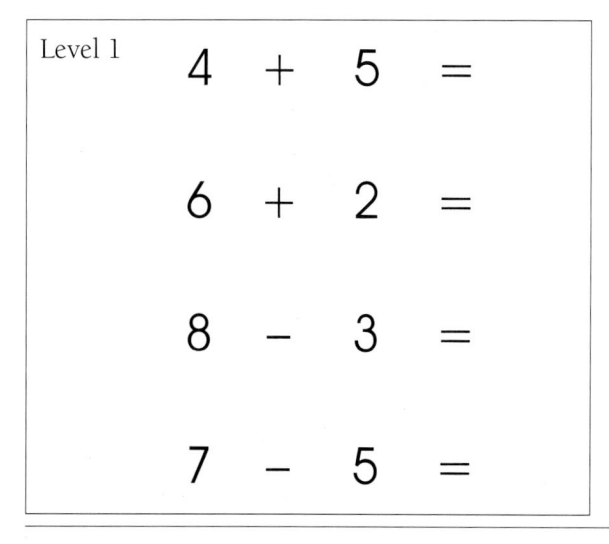

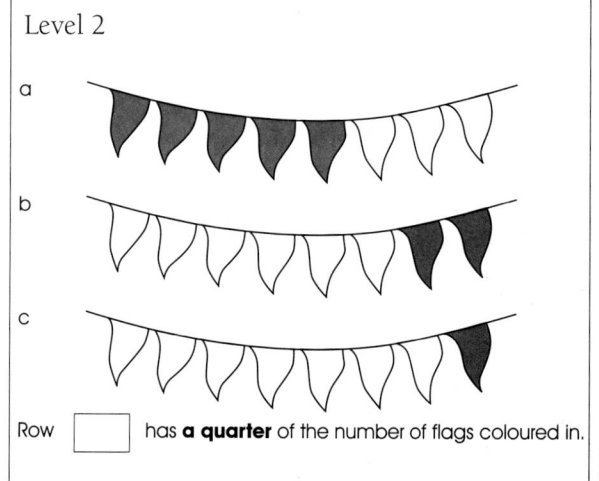

Level 1

4 + 5 =

6 + 2 =

8 - 3 =

7 - 5 =

Level 2

a
b
c

Row ☐ has **a quarter** of the number of flags coloured in.

42

Level 2

Ring Game

Some children played a game with rings.
They had two throws each.
How much did each one score?

Chris	2	and	3	_____
Sam	3	and	5	_____
Neelam	4	and	2	_____

How much **more** did **Sam** score **than Chris**? _____
How much **more** did **Sam** score **than Neelam**? _____

Level 2

Work out what goes in each box and write it in.

1, 2, 3, ☐, 5, 6

2, 1, 2, 1, ☐, 1

2, 4, ☐, 8, 10, 12

10, 9, 8, ☐, 6, 5

4 + 2 = ☐

5 − ☐ = 4

☐ + 7 = 8

☐ + 3 = 5

Level 2

Make as many patterns as you can with 8 counters and write them here.

Addition

Subtraction

Tests for Seven-Year-Olds

Mathematics Level 2

Some questions from the 1993 tests

43

Level 3

1 skipping rope   £1.25

4 skipping ropes   _____

Level 3   **The Snack Stall**

1.
2.
3.
4.
5.

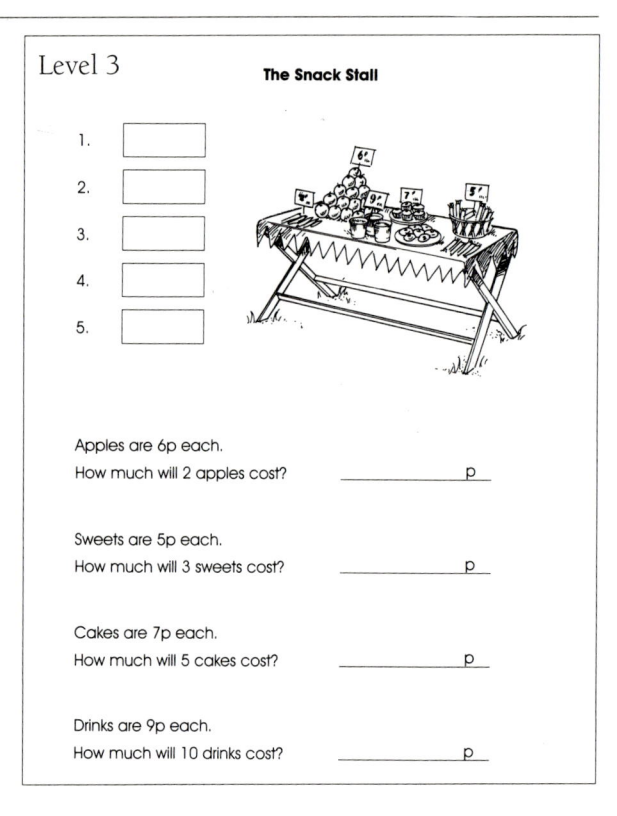

Apples are 6p each.
How much will 2 apples cost? _____ p

Sweets are 5p each.
How much will 3 sweets cost? _____ p

Cakes are 7p each.
How much will 5 cakes cost? _____ p

Drinks are 9p each.
How much will 10 drinks cost? _____ p

Level 3

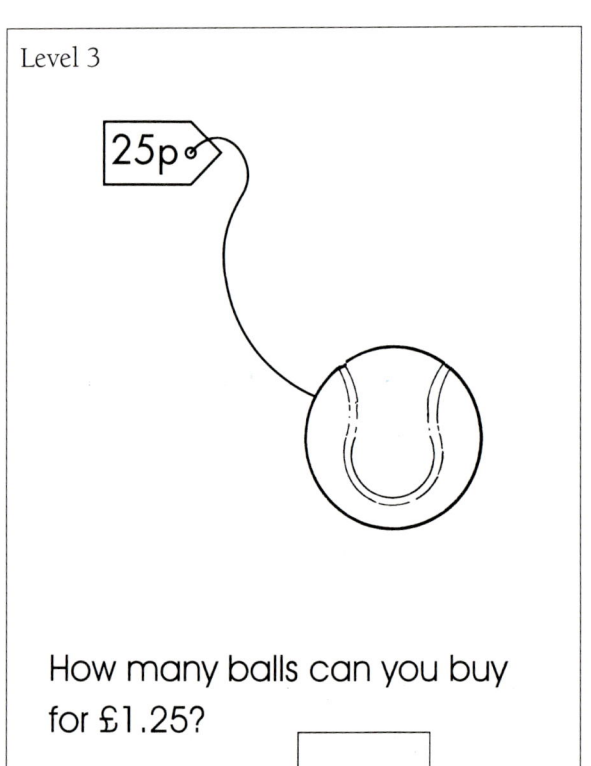

25p

How many balls can you buy for £1.25?

Tests for Seven-Year-Olds

Mathematics Level 3

Some questions from the 1993 tests

Tests for Seven-Year-Olds

Mathematics Level 4

Some questions from the 1993 tests

Level 4

Paper Cups

Cassie helped sell drinks at the fair. She sold the drinks in paper cups. The cups came in boxes. There were 15 cups in each box.

How many boxes did Cassie have to open for

90 drinks? _____

100 drinks? _____

230 drinks? _____

Level 4

Look at the numbers in these tables.
They make a lot of number patterns.

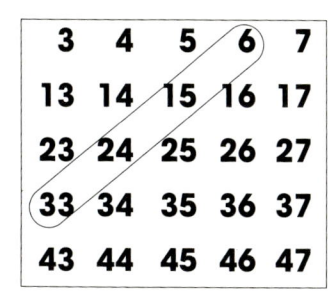

3	4	5	6	7
13	14	15	16	17
23	24	25	26	27
33	34	35	36	37
43	44	45	46	47

Explain why the numbers drawn round make a number pattern.

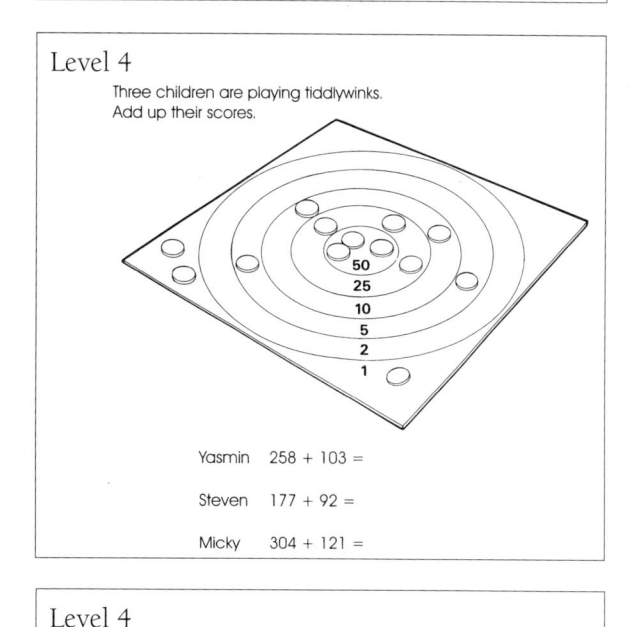

Level 4

Three children are playing tiddlywinks.
Add up their scores.

50
25
10
5
2
1

Yasmin   258 + 103 =

Steven   177 + 92 =

Micky   304 + 121 =

Level 4

Beans in a Jar

Some children are trying to guess the numbers of beans in a jar.

Here are some of the guesses they made.

Yasmin 256   Micky   942
Steven 1075   Cassie   2560

There are four numbers here. Which is the smallest? Write it down on the line and then write down the other numbers, going from the smallest to the largest number.

Level 4

After the Fair

400 people came to the fair.
What fraction of them had a go at these games?

Tiddlywinks   200 people played. $200 = \frac{1}{2}$ of 400
Hoop game   100 people played. $100 = \boxed{}$ of 400
Guess-the-beans game
                 40 people played. $40 = \boxed{}$ of 400
Drinks   300 people bought drinks.

What fraction of the people who came to the fair had drinks?

$300 = \boxed{}$ of 400

45

Science

Here and opposite are some of the questions from the 1993 tests for seven-year-olds. The questions on this page are at Level 2.

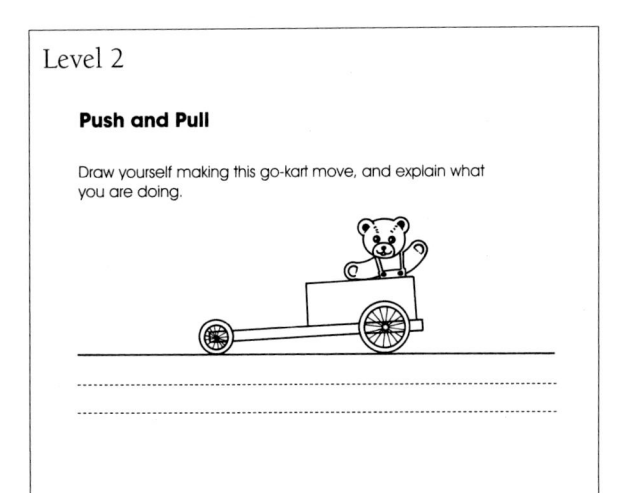

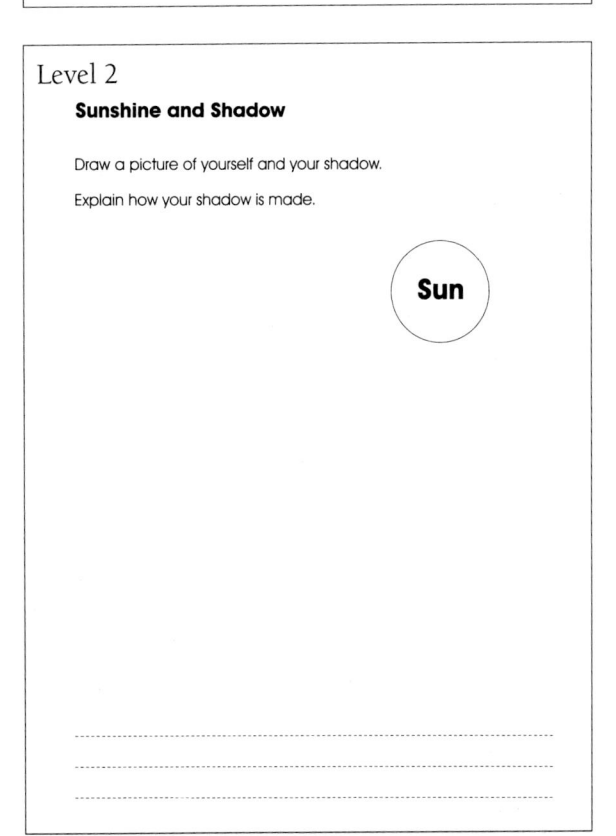

Level 2

Push and Pull

Draw yourself making this go-kart move, and explain what you are doing.

Level 2

Draw yourself making this go-kart slow down, and explain what you are doing.

Level 2

Sunshine and Shadow

Draw a picture of yourself and your shadow.

Explain how your shadow is made.

Sun

Level 2

Magnets

Here are some magnets.
Magnets attract some things.
Put **a tick** by the things magnets attract.
Put **a cross** by the things magnets will not attract.

orange   nail
jumper   flower
metal scissors brick
wooden spoon   paper clip
drawing pin   metal spoon

These two magnets are clinging together.

If one magnet is turned round and they are put together again, what happens now?

Tests for Seven-Year-Olds

Science Levels 3 and 4

Some questions from the 1993 tests

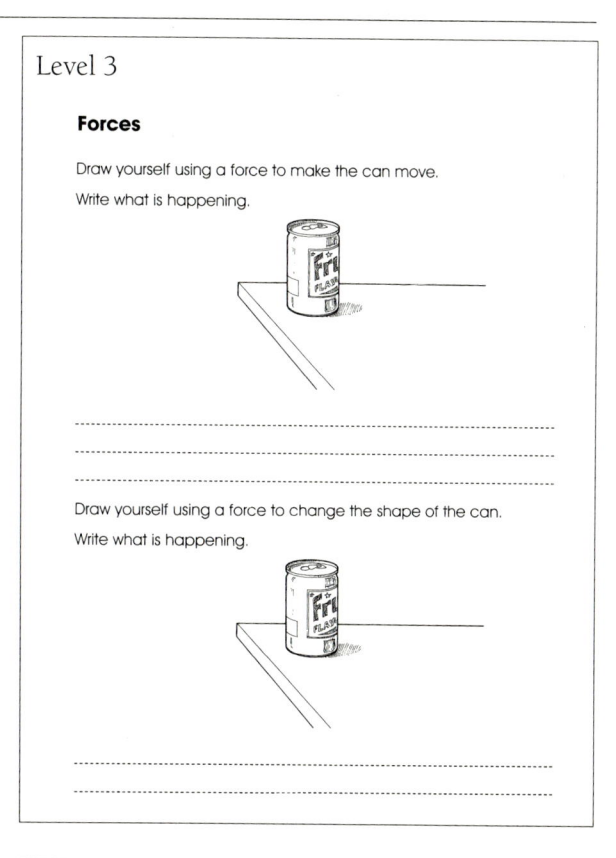

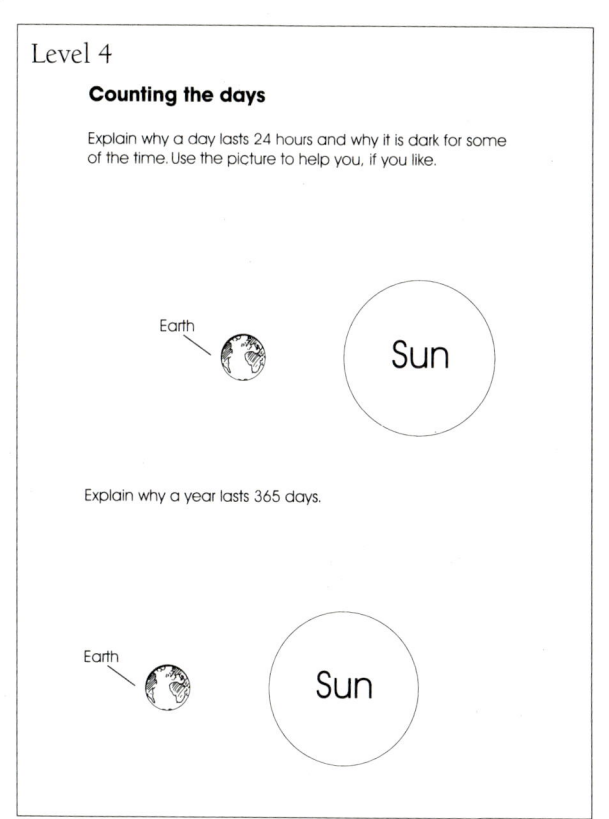

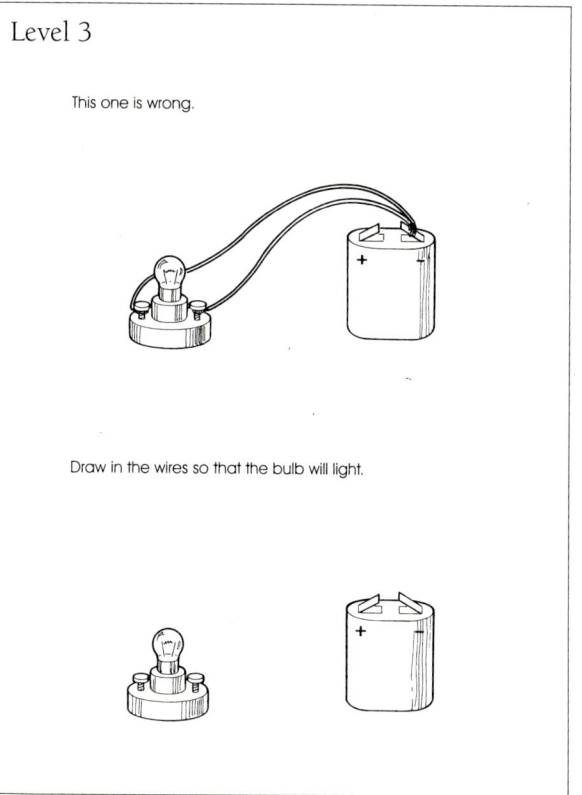

Level 3

Forces

Draw yourself using a force to make the can move.
Write what is happening.

Draw yourself using a force to change the shape of the can.
Write what is happening.

Level 4

Counting the days

Explain why a day lasts 24 hours and why it is dark for some of the time. Use the picture to help you, if you like.

Explain why a year lasts 365 days.

Level 3

This one is wrong.

Draw in the wires so that the bulb will light.

Tests for 11-Year-Olds

The tests will be taken at the end of Key Stage Two, towards the end of Year Six. Many of the children in the class are likely to be 11 and in their seventh year at primary school.

National pilot tests for 11-year-olds will be introduced for the first time in 1994 in English, mathematics and science. They will be optional but it is intended that they will become compulsory in 1995.

A few local authorities have grammar schools, which select pupils according to academic ability. They already have their own tests or assessments which are used to determine whether pupils should get places. These tests may well continue alongside the new national curriculum tests.

There is a long tradition of testing children at the age of 11. Many primary schools have their own formal tests. How far schools will continue to use these is uncertain now that the national curriculum has been introduced.

What Do the Grades Mean?

The gap between the brightest and less able pupils will be much wider for 11-year-olds. In mathematics, for example, the difference can be equivalent to seven years.

Most pupils will be expected to achieve Level 4 or above. It is anticipated that the pupil of average ability will get Level 4. Those who get Level 2 or 3 would be below average. Level 5 would be above average. Level 6 or 7 would be exceptional for 11-year-olds.

It is, again, likely that your child will achieve different levels according to the subject and even the topic within those subjects.

What Will the Tests Involve?

The exact form of the tests for 1994 has yet to be decided. However, a small number of schools did try out some experimental tests in 1993. The examples below will give you some idea of what might be expected when the final tests are produced. Chapter 2 also outlines the standards expected of pupils at the various levels.

English

Pupils judged to be between Levels 3 and 6 for reading had to read a story, 'Who's Afraid?', by Philippa Pearce, then answer questions on it. For example: Why do you think the author used the title 'Who's Afraid?'? Did you like this story? Yes/No. Why? Say what you liked or did not like about the story.

There was a separate reading test for pupils judged to be at Levels 1 or 2. In spelling, children had to fill in the words in the copy of a story read out by the teacher.

Words for Levels 1 and 2 included: went, bus, park, arrived, together, lunches, talking, edge, woods, jumped, down, big, decided, children, sun. Words for Levels 3 to 6 included: arrived, permission, prepared, because, children, together, environmental, lunches, adventure, amazingly, judging, height, brilliance, visible, journey, disappeared, straightened, suspension, descended, immediately, organised, talking.

Mathematics

Here and opposite are some questions from the 1993 pilot tests for 11-year-olds.

Level 3

There are 6 mini-rolls in each pack.

MumKnowsBest 6 Mini-Rolls

They buy 25 packs.

How many mini-rolls do they buy?

Level 3

Put a tick in the box if the sign has **reflective symmetry**.
Put a cross in the box if the sign does **not** have **reflective symmetry**.

Level 3

The children in Year 6 have been looking for shapes on the front of the school. Here are some they have found.

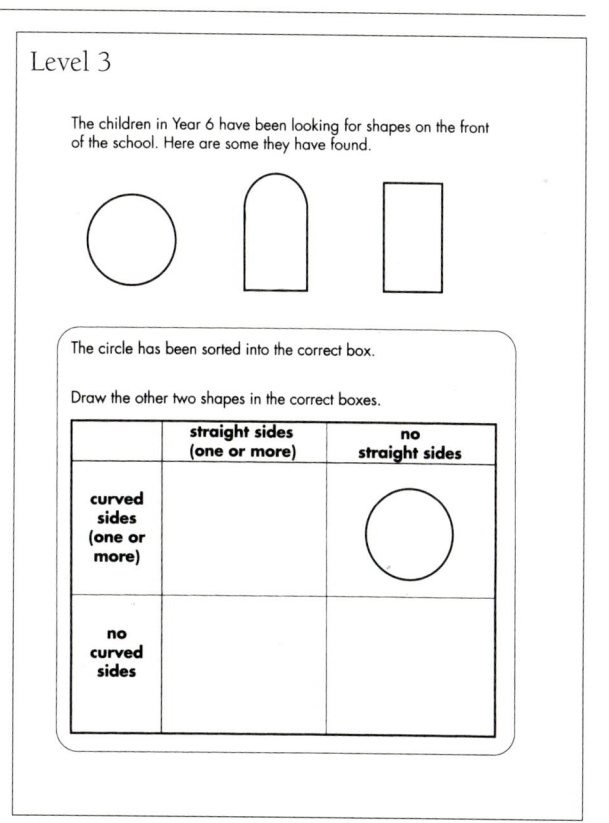

The circle has been sorted into the correct box.

Draw the other two shapes in the correct boxes.

	straight sides (one or more)	no straight sides
curved sides (one or more)		○
no curved sides		

Level 3

Ann and Rashid go to the shop to buy food for the school trip.
They walk up the street and pass these houses.

Number 519

Number 589

Number 503

Number 621

Write the four numbers in order, **smallest to largest**

smallest   largest

Tests for 11-Year-Olds

Mathematics Level 3

Some questions from the 1993 pilot tests

Level 4

THINK OF A NUMBER

Write your numbers in the boxes.

1. Think of a number between 1 and 4. ☐
2. Double your number. ☐
3. Add 3 to your last number. ☐
4. Double your last number. ☐
5. Add 2 to the last number. ☐
6. Divide the very last number by 4. ☐
7. Take away the number you started with. ☐

IS YOUR ANSWER 2? Yes or No. ☐

Level 4

THREE IN A LINE

They call out two points which are on a straight line.

Ann and Katy call out (5,1) and (1,5).

The two points have been plotted on the grid for you.

Plot a point which is in the same straight line as (5,1) and (1,5).

Write down the coordinates of your point. ☐

Level 4

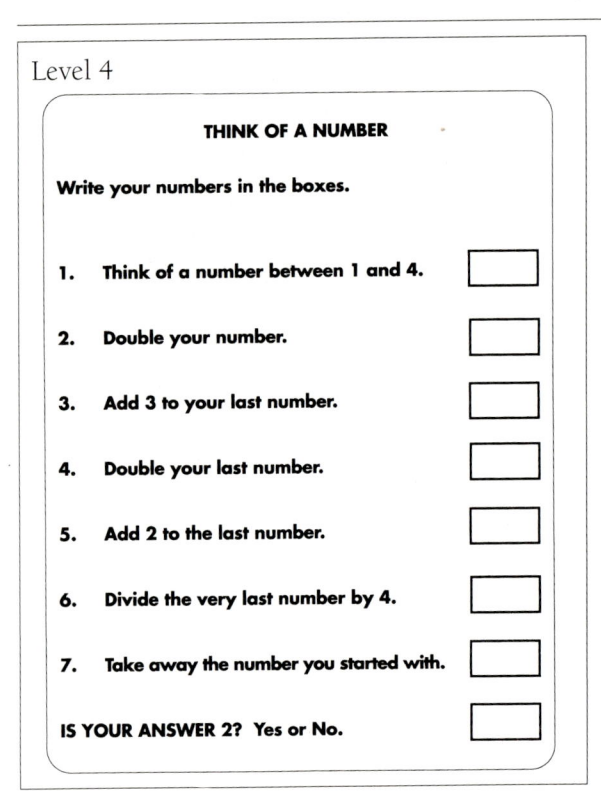

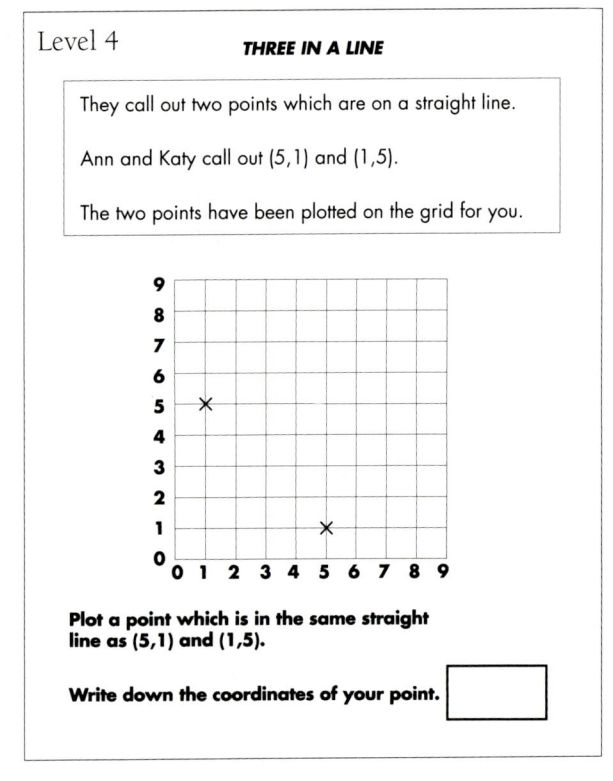

The children in Year 6 made a grid in the playground to play games.

6 metres
5 metres

They paint a line all round the edge.

How long will this be? ☐ m

What is the area of the grid? ☐ m²

Tests for 11-Year-Olds

Mathematics Level 4

Some questions from the 1993 pilot tests

Level 5

The children did a survey of the make of the cars in the car park at school.
They drew a graph of their results.

**Westwood School
cars in car park on a Monday**

- Volvo (16.7%)
- Ford (50.0%)
- Vauxhall (25%)
- Fiat (8.3%)

Which make of car has the **least** number in the car park?

There are **3 Fiats** in the car park.
How many **Fords** are there?

How many cars are there **altogether** in the car park?

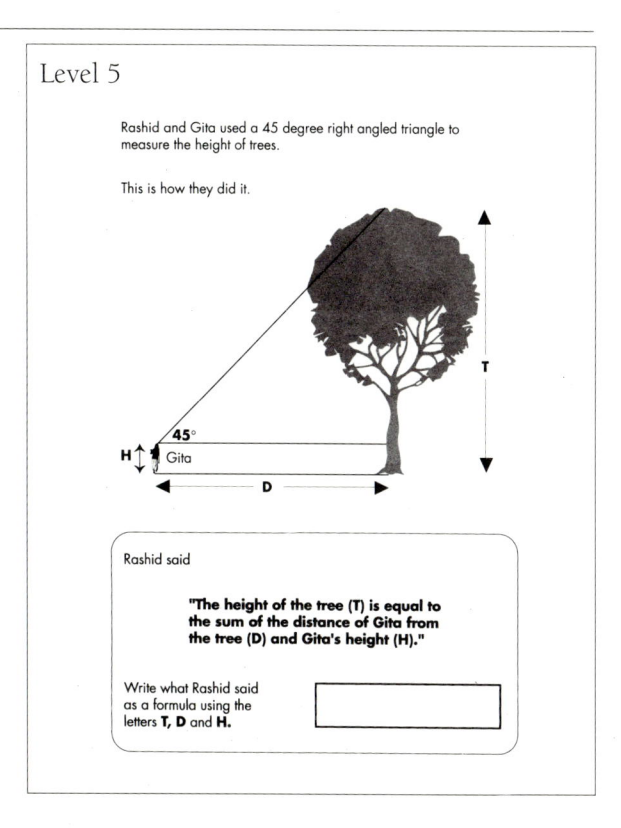

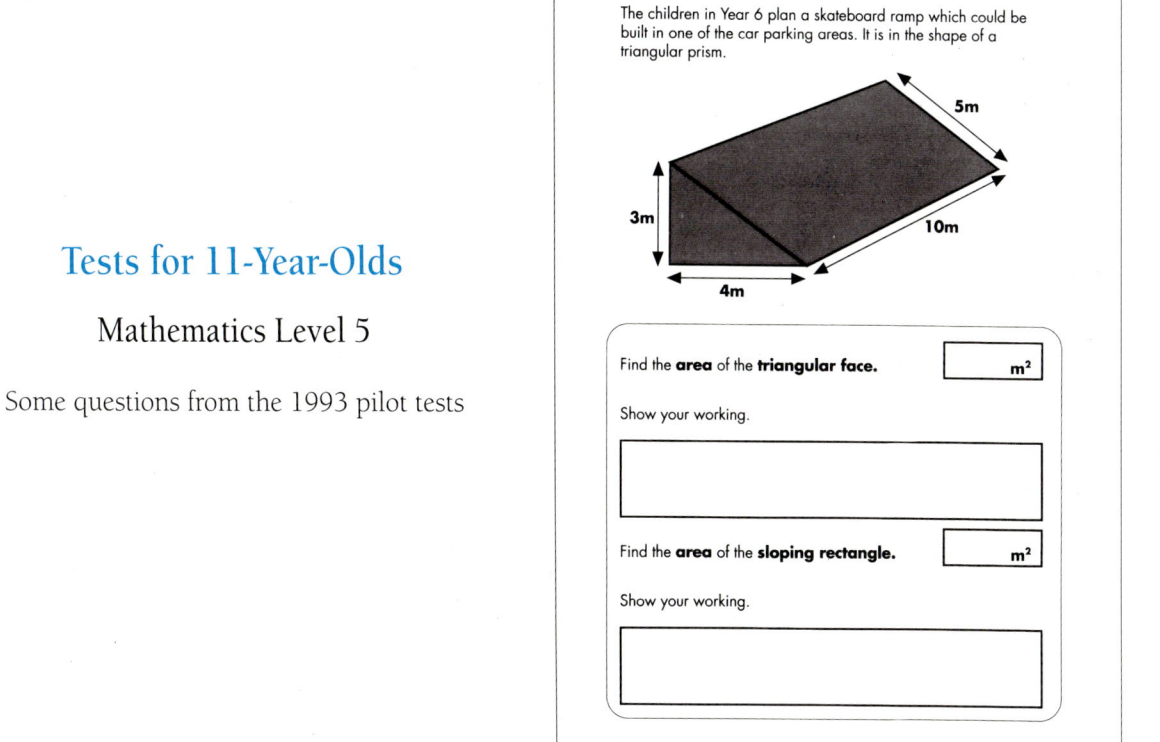

Level 5

Rashid and Gita used a 45 degree right angled triangle to measure the height of trees.

This is how they did it.

Rashid said

"The height of the tree (T) is equal to the sum of the distance of Gita from the tree (D) and Gita's height (H)."

Write what Rashid said as a formula using the letters **T, D** and **H**.

Tests for 11-Year-Olds

Mathematics Level 5

Some questions from the 1993 pilot tests

Level 5

The children in Year 6 plan a skateboard ramp which could be built in one of the car parking areas. It is in the shape of a triangular prism.

5m, 3m, 10m, 4m

Find the **area** of the **triangular face**. m^2

Show your working.

Find the **area** of the **sloping rectangle**. m^2

Show your working.

51

Level 6

Here is a table of the length and area of squares to help calculate the amount of lawn seed needed to make a school lawn.

length (L) of side in metres	area (A) of square in square metres
1	1
2	4
3	9
4	16
5	25
6	36

Three of the six points have been plotted on the coordinate grid.

Complete by plotting the remaining points.

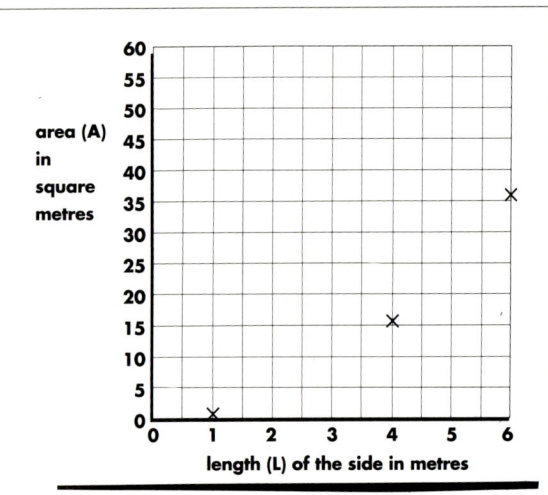

Draw the graph of $A = L^2$

Use your graph to find the area of a square of side length 3.5 metres. ☐ m²

Draw on your graph to show how this can be worked out.

Test for 11-Year-Olds

Mathematics Levels 6

Some questions from the 1993 pilot tests

Level 6

The radius of the 'No Parking' sign is 7 cm.

Use π on your calculator or take $\pi = \frac{22}{7}$

What is the circumference of the sign? ☐ cm

What is the area of the sign? ☐ cm²

Use this space for your working

Science

Here and overleaf are some of the questions from the 1993 pilot tests for 11-year-olds. The questions on this page are at Level 3.

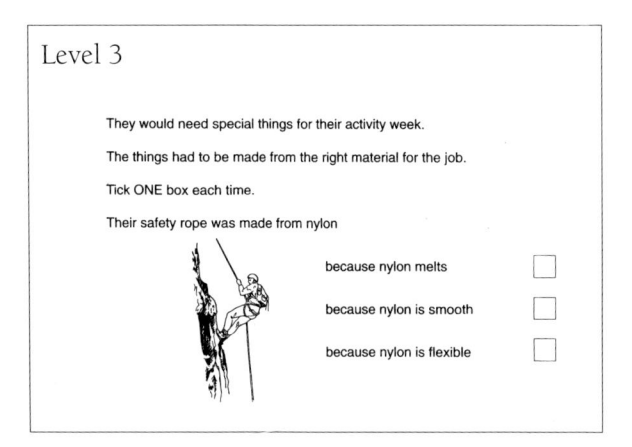

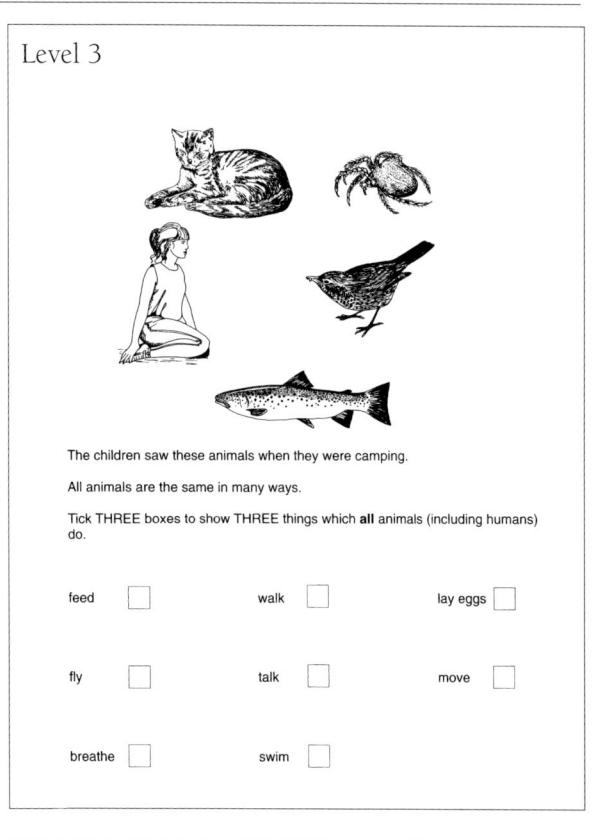

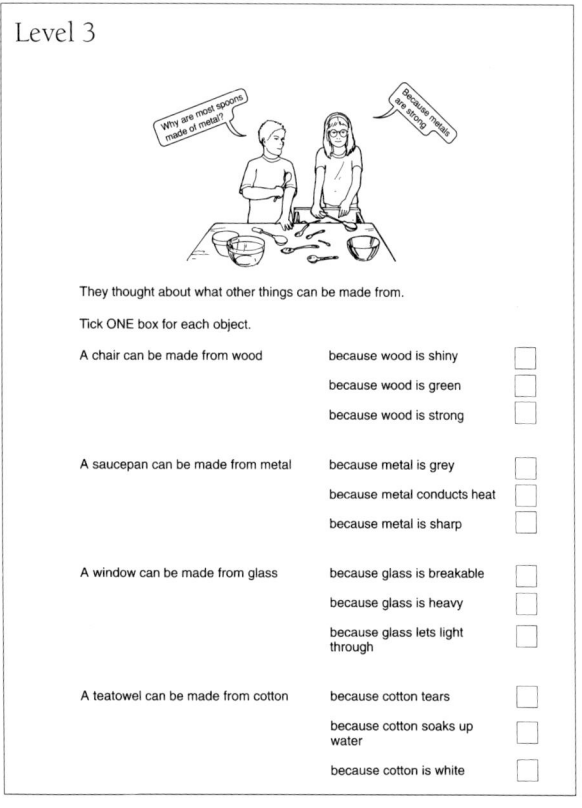

Level 3

They would need special things for their activity week.

The things had to be made from the right material for the job.

Tick ONE box each time.

Their safety rope was made from nylon

- because nylon melts ☐
- because nylon is smooth ☐
- because nylon is flexible ☐

Level 3

The children saw these animals when they were camping.

All animals are the same in many ways.

Tick THREE boxes to show THREE things which **all** animals (including humans) do.

feed ☐	walk ☐	lay eggs ☐
fly ☐	talk ☐	move ☐
breathe ☐	swim ☐	

Level 3

One group went for a walk.

Sam saw rocks with cracks in.

Some bits of rock had fallen onto the path.

'I bet walkers and animals did that', said Sam.

'The weather can crack and break rocks', added the leader.

How can the weather weaken the rock and make pieces break off?

....
....
....

Level 3

"Why are most spoons made of metal?"
"Because metals are strong"

They thought about what other things can be made from.

Tick ONE box for each object.

A chair can be made from wood
- because wood is shiny ☐
- because wood is green ☐
- because wood is strong ☐

A saucepan can be made from metal
- because metal is grey ☐
- because metal conducts heat ☐
- because metal is sharp ☐

A window can be made from glass
- because glass is breakable ☐
- because glass is heavy ☐
- because glass lets light through ☐

A teatowel can be made from cotton
- because cotton tears ☐
- because cotton soaks up water ☐
- because cotton is white ☐

Level 4

They wanted to cook a hot meal.

They could use one of these to cook their food:

wood fire   gas stove   paraffin stove.

Choose one of these.

What is the source of energy in the cooker you have chosen?
....

How is the energy released?
....

Name a waste gas given off from the cooker as it heats the food.
....

Level 4

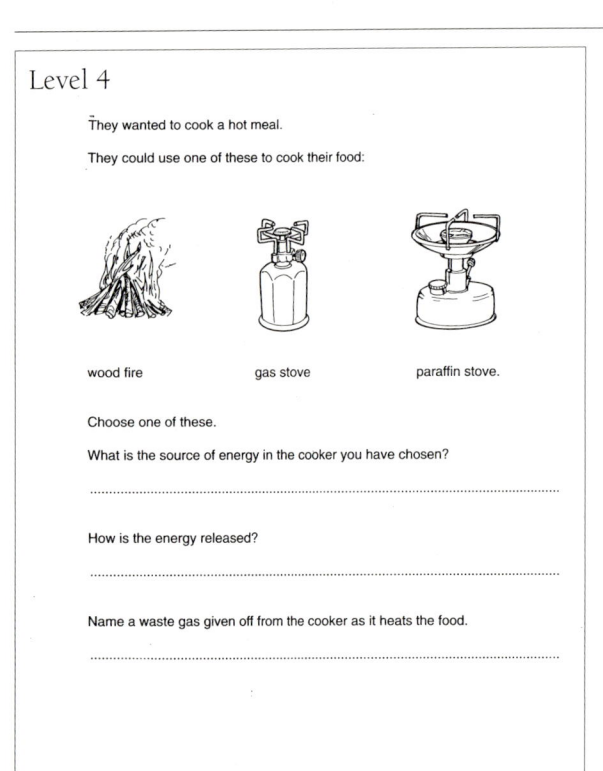

blue tits: eat insects and caterpillars

hedgehogs: eat roots, berries, insects

rabbits: eat leaves and grass

moles: eat worms

caterpillars: eat leaves

sparrowhawks: eat small birds

Complete the food chain. Draw **or** write in the three boxes below.

☐ → ☐ → ☐ → sparrowhawk

Grass and trees are producers in a food chain. Explain what a producer is.

Tests for 11-Year-Olds

Science Levels 4 and 5

Some questions from the 1993 pilot tests

Level 5

Dad was making a meal.

Suddenly, the chip pan fat caught fire!

Dad switched off the electric cooker.

What should he do next?

Tick ONE box only.

Take the pan off the heat and blow the flames	Take the pan outside	Put the lid on the pan
A ☐	B ☐	C ☐

Explain why he should do this, in terms of the gas involved.

Tests for 14-Year-Olds

National tests for 14-year-olds in 1993 took the form of short, written 'examination' papers that all pupils in Year Nine in England and Wales were scheduled to sit at the same time on the same day. However, the paperwork and bureaucracy that accompanied them led to criticism that they imposed an unreasonable workload on teachers. There were also complaints about their quality. The resulting boycott by the three main teaching unions meant that few pupils sat them.

Tests for 14-year-olds in mathematics and science were piloted in 1992 and a significant number of schools volunteered to take part in the exercise. It is the tests in English and technology introduced nationally in 1993 that have been more controversial.

What Do the Grades Mean?

The differences in the achievement of pupils at the age of 14 is so wide that the brightest could get Level 10 and the least able could get Level 1. This is why there are different papers for pupils of different abilities. The child of average ability would be expected to get a Level 6 or a Level 7. Level 8 is above average. Levels 9 or 10 represent exceptional achievement. Most pupils will be between Levels 5 and 8. It is, again, likely that your child will achieve different levels according to the subject and even the topic within those subjects.

What Will the Tests Involve?

The exact form of the tests has yet to be decided. The examples from the tests for 1993 are only pointers to the things that your child would be expected to know and be able to do at the age of 14.

English

Pupils at Levels 3 to 5 had to write 300 words on one topic, chosen from a list of four – for example, 'Write about a time when you had to make a difficult choice, **or** Write about a time when a problem was unexpectedly solved.' Two of the questions included photographs – for example, 'Write a story which has the title "The End is at Hand". You may use one of the people in the picture on page 4 as the main character in your story if you wish.'

Mathematics

Here is a question from the 1993 tests aimed at pupils at Levels 5 to 8.

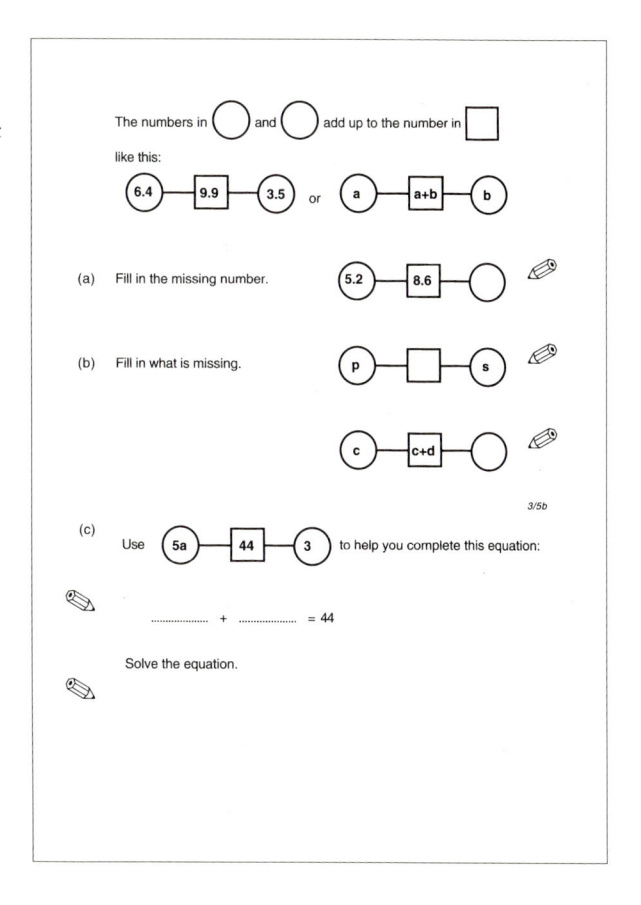

The numbers in ◯ and ◯ add up to the number in ▢ like this:

$6.4 \to 9.9 \to 3.5$ or $a \to a+b \to b$

(a) Fill in the missing number. $5.2 \to 8.6 \to \bigcirc$

(b) Fill in what is missing.

$p \to \square \to s$

$c \to c+d \to \bigcirc$

(c) Use $5a \to 44 \to 3$ to help you complete this equation:

.... + ... = 44

Solve the equation.

Science

Here is a question from the 1993 tests aimed at pupils at Level 5 to 8.

Three different fuels were investigated.

Each liquid fuel was used to heat 50 g samples of water in a beaker.

The table shows the results of burning **three** 1 g samples of different liquid fuels.

liquid fuel sample	starting temperature of water in °C	final temperature of water in °C
A	20	40
B	22	40
C	18	36

(a) Which **one** of the three liquid fuel samples produced the most exothermic reaction?

_____

(b) Explain what is meant by 'exothermic'.

_____
_____

The GCSE

The GCSE examination was introduced in schools and colleges in 1986 to replace O-levels and CSEs. Candidates sat the first GCSEs in the summer of 1988. It is designed to be an examination for children of all abilities. In the past, only the more academically able pupils were allowed to take O-levels. Less able children sat CSEs. This was felt to be divisive.

Nearly all children will take GCSEs. Only those judged to be at Levels 1 to 3 in the national curriculum are unlikely to sit GCSEs. However, their final reports from school will still detail their achievements and the levels they have reached.

GCSE courses generally last two years and are taken at the end of Key Stage Four (Year 11) when most pupils are aged 15 or 16.

It is important to remember that GCSE is very different from the old O-Level, which was a traditional examination that tested pupils' ability to learn and remember a set amount of knowledge. The GCSE reflects changes in teaching styles that have put more emphasis on teaching children skills as much as knowledge. It aims to test what they can do and know rather than penalising them for what they don't know.

What Do the Grades Mean?

Candidates are graded from A to G. Below that there is a U, which stands for ungraded or unclassified. Most candidates will gain at least one GCSE. In 1992, more than 91% of all pupils got at least one GCSE at a G grade or above. The higher grades of A, B and C are sometimes described as 'pass' grades. They are designed to be broadly equivalent to the old O-Level pass grades of A, B and C.

Pupils who get four or more GCSEs at grades A to C are in a strong position to go on to do A-levels. More than 38% of pupils gained five or more GCSEs at grades A to C in 1992.

The table below shows the GCSE pass rates for that year. The figures do not include children who were not able to sit any GCSEs.

GCSE Pass Rates (1992)

GCSE Grade	% of Candidates
A	15.2
B	16.7
C	21.9
D	17.7
E	13.5
F	8.8
G	4.6
U	1.6
A to C	53.8
A to G	98.4

The table on page 57 shows the GCSE pass rates for English, English literature, mathematics and science. The percentages represent the proportion of candidates in each subject gaining each of the grades.

GCSE Pass Rates (1992)

Subject	A	B	C	D	E	F	G	U	A to C	A to G	
English	9.6	17.7	28	22	13.5	6.7	2.1	0.4	55.3	99.6	%
English Literature	12	19.9	27.2	20.1	12.8	5.9	1.6	0.5	59.1	99.5	%
Maths	9	10.5	25.9	17.7	17.5	11.7	4.8	2.9	45.4	97.1	%
Science	9.4	12.2	22.3	20.5	16.5	11.2	5.6	2.3	43.9	97.7	%

In 1994 and subsequent years, the government is to introduce a 'starred' A grade, which is sometimes described as a super A grade. It is for those candidates with the best A grades and will reward exceptional achievement.

There are six examining groups who are responsible for setting and marking the papers. They have to draw up and mark the examinations in accordance with national guidelines. That means that wherever you are in the country, the grade that your child achieves will be equivalent to the same grade in another area.

The six groups are:

- University of London Examinations and Assessment Council (ULEAC)

- Midland Examining Group (MEG)

- Northern Examinations and Assessment Board (NEAB)

- Northern Ireland Schools Examination Council (NISEC)

- Southern Examining Group (SEG)

- Welsh Joint Education Committee (WJEC)

Your child's school is likely to 'shop' around between the boards to find a syllabus that they feel is appropriate for their pupils in particular subjects. If your school is in the south of the country, there is nothing to stop it from choosing the northern board.

How Important Is Coursework?

Coursework is still an important part of GCSE courses. It gives pupils a chance to broaden their studies by going into a particular topic or issue in more depth. It also allows pupils greater freedom to choose what they will study. This improves children's motivation and is one of the reasons why it is supported by many teachers.

Nearly all syllabuses contain some coursework. This means that pupils may have a number of projects on the go at the same time. If they feel snowed under by the amount of work, they should speak to their teachers.

There used to be GCSE courses where all the marks were awarded on the basis of coursework. The new limits, introduced by the government, mean that in nearly all courses no more than 40% of the marks will be awarded for coursework.

Tiered Papers

As with other tests for older children, pupils of different abilities will take different papers. There are three or four tiers of papers in a number of subjects. The hardest papers might allow a child to get any grade between A and D inclusive. The middle tier might allow them to achieve any grade between C and F. The lowest tier might be for grades E to G. This is not a definitive model for tiered papers. There are variations.

Spelling, Punctuation and Grammar

New requirements have been introduced which mean that up to 5% of the marks in all GCSE subjects can be lost for poor spelling, punctuation and grammar.

The rule applies to both coursework and written examinations. In science subjects, where there is less writing, it will have less of an effect.

School Reports and League Tables

Parents must by law receive a school report containing their child's GCSE results as well as any other qualifications.

The report will enable you to make comparisons between your child's performance and that of other pupils in the school and nationally. The information will be presented in a standard format.

The overall results of the pupils in the school, in the education authority and in the country as a whole also have to be published in the school's prospectus and in its annual governors' report to parents. Performance tables of the GCSE results from every secondary school in each of the local education authorities throughout England and Wales are published in November by the Department for Education. These will also include schools' A-level results if they have a sixth form.

A-Levels

Nearly a quarter of all pupils now go on to get at least one A-level. That compares with one in six at the beginning of the 1970s.

The courses are provided by eight examining boards in England and Wales. Like GCSE, the boards have to follow national guidelines which ensure that grades are consistent across the country.

Your child's school or college is likely to run courses from a few of the boards at most. This may restrict choice since not all the boards offer all the 60-plus subjects that are available at A-level.

The combinations of A-levels that can be chosen will also depend on the school's timetable, staffing and resources. If there is a course or combination of A-levels that your child particularly wants to study, it may be worth investigating whether it is available at another nearby college.

What Do the Grades Mean?

A-levels are graded from A to E. Below that, there is an 'N', which essentially means that the candidate nearly got an A-level. In the past, N used to be classified as equivalent to an old O-level pass. Below that, there is a 'U', which is unclassified or fail.

Students who get two or three A-levels stand a good chance of getting a place at university. The 'established' universities will generally require higher grades for most courses and particularly for those in the arts and social sciences.

The 'new' universities, which used to be known as polytechnics, often have a wider range of courses including more vocational, job-related options.

Between 10% and 20% of candidates achieve an A grade, depending on the subject. Nearly half get one of the three top grades of A, B and C.

The table on page 59 shows the proportion of candidates getting each grade in seven of the most popular subjects in 1992, the most recent year for

A-Level Pass Rates (1992)

Grade	A	B	C	D	E	N	U
Subject (number of candidates)							
English (86,779)	11.2	17.7	20	21	16.6	8	5.5 %
French (31,261)	17.6	17.3	19	18.4	14.4	8	5.3 %
History (46,698)	11.6	17.2	19.2	19.2	15.1	9	8.8 %
Mathematics (72,384)	20.1	14.6	14.2	14	13	10	14.1 %
Physics (41,301)	15.1	15.5	15.8	16.6	15.4	10.9	10.6 %
Chemistry (42,697)	16.1	18.3	16.2	15.8	14	9.6	10 %
Biology (48,742)	12.4	15.2	16.5	17.5	16.1	11.2	11.2 %

which figures are available.

The A-level results of pupils are often presented in terms of points scores. The method is often used for university entrance. The government's performance tables of school results also use the same official formula.

It is a straightforward calculation where each grade at A-level, or at A/S level, is worth a certain number of points: an A grade at A-level is worth 10 points; B = eight points; C = six points; D = four points; E = two points.

An A grade at A/S level is worth five points; B = four points; C = three points; D = two points; E = one point.

See the section on choices at 16 in Chapter 4 for further information about A-levels.

Appeals Against Grades

A candidate can appeal against his or her grades in a public examination (including GCSE and A-level) if there is evidence of an error. However, this can only be done through the school or college.

It may be that the school supports the case that the examining board is at fault. If it doesn't, the school can charge you for the cost of a re-mark of the papers by the examination board.

If a GCSE or A-level examination board concludes that there wasn't a mistake, you can go further and appeal to the Independent Appeals Authority of Schools Examinations (IAASE). However, the authority will only hear an appeal if it is backed by the candidate's school or college.

Further information is available from: The Secretary of the IAASE, Newcombe House, 45 Notting Hill Gate, London W11 3JB. Tel: 071-229-1234.

Parents' Rights

No charges can be made for entering pupils for public examinations that are set out in official regulations. The school will have a full list of the examinations, which include GCSE, A-levels and vocational courses.

A school must enter a pupil for each examination syllabus for which the child has been prepared by the teachers. The only exception is if the head teacher feels that there is a good educational reason not to enter the pupil or if the parents ask in writing that the child should not be entered.

An examination entry fee may only be charged to parents if:

- The candidate was not prepared for the examination at the school where the pupil is taking it.

- The examination is not on the set list but the school arranges for the pupil to take it.

- A pupil fails without good reason to complete the studies for the examination.

6
Choosing A School

Parents are entitled to a free school place for their child from the age of five to 16, and a place at a school or college from 16 to 18. The education of children at 'maintained' or 'state' schools is paid for by the taxpayer. Parents have a duty to ensure that their child gets an education. A few parents teach their children at home but the local education authority has to be satisfied about the standards. By law, children cannot leave school until they are 16.

What Sort of Schools Are There?

Children will generally be in **primary school** at the age of five. Many will remain in the same school until they reach the age of 11 when they will move on to **secondary school.**

In some areas, primary schools are divided into **infants schools**, which generally teach children from the age of five to seven, and **junior schools** for pupils aged seven to 11. Infant and junior schools may be combined on one large site or they may be separated by some distance.

Some local education authorities have different starting ages for secondary school. It may be at 12, 13 or even 14. A few areas operate a three-tier system where pupils start in **first schools** from five until eight or nine, then move on to **middle schools** before joining **high schools** at the age of 12 or 13.

There are also different types of state school:

County Schools are the ultimate responsibility of the local education authority. The size of the school's budget is decided by the authority but the school's head teacher and governors are in charge of how that money is spent within the school. They are also in charge of how the school is run although the local authority offers advice and can step in if there are problems.

Voluntary Schools are under the control of voluntary or charitable bodies. In most cases, these will be the Roman Catholic church or the Church of England. The churches still contribute some money towards the school but most of the funds come from the state.

Grant-Maintained Schools are schools that have opted out of their local education authority's control and receive their funds directly from the Department for Education. Most are secondary schools, although there are a growing number of primary schools. They are run entirely by the governors and head teachers and are independent of the local authority.

Comprehensive Schools accept children of all abilities. More than nine in 10 schools are comprehensive whether they are county, voluntary or grant-maintained.

Grammar Schools select children at the age of 11 on the basis of their academic ability. Pupils may be selected through special tests, interviews and reports from their primary schools. There are about 150 grammar schools across the country. Pupils who fail to get into grammar schools will go to neighbouring Secondary Modern Schools.

City Technology Colleges (CTCs) are new types of schools that have been set up in urban areas and are funded by the government and by business. They are free, cater for pupils of all abilities and place a special emphasis on teaching science and technology. There are now 15 CTCs.

Independent Schools number about 2500 and generally require parents to pay fees. About 600,000 pupils attend independent schools, accounting for 7.5% of all children aged 5 to 18. There is a scheme whereby pupils aged 11 to 18 can have part or all of their fees paid by the government. About 31,500 children aged 11 to 18 attend nearly 300 independent schools under what is called the Assisted Places Scheme (APS).

All state schools, whatever their type, have to follow the national curriculum. Only independent schools are exempt.

What to Look For in a Good School

Educationists have spent years trying to answer this question. What follows can only be a pointer to some of the factors that researchers and inspectors have identified.

A Good Head Teacher who offers strong leadership, motivates staff and is accessible to teachers and parents.

Good Relations Between Head Teacher and Staff. All the teachers agree on the aims of the school and work to achieve them.

A Well-Qualified Staff who have consistent approaches to teaching. There will be little variation in standards between different subjects.

High Expectations for all pupils from the most able to the least able. Pupils at the top are set work that is challenging. They are not held back or bored while less able pupils are given work suited to their abilities.

Well-Organised Lessons prepared in advance. Teachers and children arrive on time for classes.

Consistent and Regular Marking of pupils' work with detailed records kept on each child's progress.

Positive Feedback for Pupils when they do well.

The Head Teacher and Staff are not overburdened by bureaucracy and paperwork.

Strong Links with Parents, including an effective system for hearing and responding to parents' concerns. There are regular reports on pupils' progress with detailed comments and grades.

Consistently Enforced School Rules. Arbitrary discipline is a sign of a bad school.

Homework is regularly set and marked, starting by at least the age of nine.

A Wide Range of Extra-Curricular Activities from sports and visits out of school to clubs in music and drama.

Special Support for children who may be struggling.

Pupils Are Given Responsibility. Senior pupils are appointed monitors or prefects.

Well-Maintained School Buildings and Classrooms free of graffiti and litter. Even if the school is short of funds and housed in old or temporary buildings, it should be clean and tidy.

Is There Real Freedom of Choice?

The vast majority of parents get the school of their choice, although some schools are so popular that this is not always possible.

The law gives you a right to say which school you would prefer for your child. However, this doesn't mean that you are guaranteed a place at that school. Your application may be rejected if:

- The school is full to capacity with pupils who have a stronger claim on places. Schools use set criteria to decide who should get a place if they are full.

- Your child fails the entrance examination for a grammar school. This should only affect applicants for the few secondary schools that still select pupils by ability.

- Your child fails to meet the admission requirements of a voluntary church school. Church schools are entitled to limit the number of pupils from other faiths or denominations.

The more popular a school, the more likely it is to be full or oversubscribed. A school or the local education authority may be able to tell you whether it has been oversubscribed in previous years.

Some authorities include details about grant-maintained schools in their area. If they don't, the information should be available at local libraries. Useful reference books include *The Longman Education Year Book* (Longman Group UK Ltd), which lists secondary schools for each education authority, and *The Primary Education Directory* and *The Education Authorities Directory*, both produced by the School Government Publishing Company Ltd.

Grant-maintained schools have control over their own admissions, so you will have to apply direct to those schools. They have to publish their admissions criteria and all the other information necessary for parents to submit applications.

Choosing A Primary School

Some parts of the country have large numbers of children in nursery schools or nursery classes attached to a primary school. This often means that children will move on to a particular primary school. If this is the case, then decisions about the choice of a primary school may have to be taken earlier.

Different local education authorities and even individual schools have different policies as to the age at which children start school. In some, it will be the term in which they are five. That means they may start at the beginning of any of the three school terms. Others admit children once a year.

Details about nursery provision in your area

and the policies about when children start primary school will be available from your local education authority or from the schools.

Finding a School

A local education authority must publish information about schools and their admission criteria at least six weeks before the date when parents have to submit applications.

These booklets can be obtained from your local education authority. They will include basic information about schools in the area. You don't have to choose the school nearest to your home. Parents are also entitled to apply to schools outside their local authority area. If you wish to exercise that right, you should contact the neighbouring education authority to get information about their schools. This is more likely to be an option in big cities.

The education authority should also publish information about school transport, children's entitlement to free school meals, school transfers and the complaints procedures.

Getting More Information

There are three other sources of information about schools: prospectuses, the governors' annual report and reports by government inspectors. These have to be obtained in most cases from the school, although some education authorities do publish them.

You may have heard stories about local schools but it is always advisable to take such comments with a pinch of salt. The views of parents with children at the school are more valuable than local gossip, which may be inaccurate and some years out of date.

Prospectuses

Information should include at the least:

- Names of the head teacher, teaching staff and the governors.

- The type of school and any religious connections.

- The length of the school day.

- Dates for each term and half-term.

- The school's policies on homework, discipline, school uniform, charging for extra activities, pastoral care and how it covers sex education.

- Information on pupils' attendance rates.

- A summary of its curriculum and what children will be taught in each year.

- How it caters for children with special educational needs.

- Its curriculum aims.

- Arrangements for complaining if parents are dissatisfied with what their children are being taught.

Governors' Annual Reports

Information should include.

- Names of all the governors.

- A summary of the school's budget.

- Details of work by the governors to strengthen the school's links with the community.

School Inspectors' Reports

Reports by Her Majesty's Inspectorate (HMI government inspectors) on individual schools have been published irregularly for the past 20 years. The government has, however, reformed the system so that from autumn 1994 each primary school will be inspected every four years.

The new reports will present information about the school in a standard format. All parents with a child at the school should receive a summary, while the school has to make a copy available for public inspection. There may be a charge for photocopying.

You should be able to find out about government inspectors' reports and whether they are available by contacting the schools, the local education authority or Ofsted, Inspectors' Reports, Elizabeth House, York Road, London SE1 7PH. Tel: 071-925-6742

Making Your Application

Once you have decided which school or schools you are interested in, you should request an application form from them. The forms will often allow you to state a preference giving your first, second and perhaps other choices.

Take account of admissions criteria and how popular schools are when you decide your preferences. Applying for a popular school some distance from your home may put you at a disadvantage in the competition for places. In most cases, a first choice from another parent will take precedence over a second choice even if the school of your second choice is nearby.

Some local education authorities deal with applications themselves. In other cases, you will have to submit the application to the school of your first choice.

Visiting a School

Nothing beats visiting a school to help you and your child reach a decision. Prospectuses, reports and statistics are useful sources of information, but a visit will give you just as good (if not a better) sense of the school. Don't hesitate to visit half a dozen schools, or more, if you have the time and want to get a full picture of what is available in your area.

Schools should be willing to arrange visits or appointments to give you a chance to look round and meet the head teacher and some of the staff. Many also have parents' evenings and open days for prospective parents.

You will get a better impression of a school if you visit while the pupils are there. This should give you a chance to talk to the staff and children, and to see how pupils behave, work and are taught.

Questions to Ask

Most teachers will be willing to talk to you. The views of children at the school can also be a useful guide. Prospectuses and other reports offer basic information but more can be gleaned from discussions with the head teacher, staff, parents and pupils.

Here are a few ideas for issues that you might consider:

- How popular is the school?

- How much time is the school able to devote to the basics of reading, writing and mathematics?

- What is the school's approach to teaching reading, writing, spelling and mathematics?

- What is offered through the national curriculum? Are there any additional activities or subjects?

- What is the school's attitude to testing? Are there additional tests beyond those required by the national curriculum?

- What approaches does the school have to teaching? Are children of the same age taught in the same class, or are pupils of different ages taught in the same class? Are children taught in groups according to their ability?

- What is the size of the school's classes? The average size of a primary school class in England is 27 pupils. Research suggests that children in smaller classes do get a head start, although the evidence is not clear cut.

- What are the school's rules on behaviour and discipline?

- What are the attendance rates of pupils?

- What is the policy on school uniform? How much does it cost? Are there any funds available if parents can't afford the cost?

- Is homework set? At what age and how regularly?

- Does the school have any shortages of staff? How long have the staff and the head teacher been at the school? Do they plan to stay?

- Does the school offer any special assistance to children who might be struggling?

- How does the school cater for children with special talents or educational needs?

- Are there clubs or societies for pupils? What extra-curricular activities are provided?

- What is the provision in art, music, drama and sport?

- Are school meals provided? What is the quality and variety of food on offer?

- How involved are parents in the school? Is there a parent–teacher association?

- What secondary school do most of the children go on to?

What about League Tables?

The government has proposed that performance tables of each school's results in the tests for seven-year-olds should be published. The boycott by the teaching unions made it impossible to compile comprehensive tables for 1993. If the tables go ahead in 1994, they will provide parents with results from all of the primary schools in their area in the 'core' subjects of English, mathematics and science.

Any tables that are published need to be treated with caution. The results can differ significantly if a lot of the pupils in the school do not speak English at home, or if they have had the advantage of a nursery education or started at one school earlier than at another.

Choosing a Secondary School

Most parents start to consider the choice of secondary school by the time their child is aged eight or nine, in the fourth year of primary school. Although the decision does not have to be taken until the final year, it is never too early to start investigating the options.

Most primary schools have strong links with secondary schools. Some primaries are often described as 'feeder' schools to a secondary school in their area, having traditionally sent large numbers of pupils to that particular school.

Good primary schools will often invite teachers from the local secondaries to explain to their final-year children what to expect when they transfer. Many arrange visits to secondary schools, which also generally hold open days and evenings for prospective parents and pupils. As the time for transfer approaches, children may have a few lessons at the secondary school to help make the move less daunting. They may also be set tasks to do in preparation for their arrival.

The head teacher at your child's primary school is likely to play an important part in your decision. The head teacher can explain the process for transfer to secondary school and may be able to give you some idea about which school he or she thinks would be best for your child.

Finding a School

Booklets and information about all the secondary schools in your local authority area are provided in the same way as for primary schools. They will be available from the authority. Some distribute them to primary schools. Grant-maintained schools may not be included in the booklets. So, again, you can check in the local library.

The formal process of choosing a secondary school is likely to begin in the winter term, shortly after your child starts their final year in primary school. There are a number of basic factors that may need to be considered.

Travelling to School. The first factor is the distance that your child may have to travel. The rules on entitlement to free school transport are the same as for primary: you don't have to choose the nearest school. But if the nearest school is not within walking distance (three miles for children aged over eight), the education authority must provide free transport.

Options at 16. You may also have to take some account of your child's options at the age of 16. For example, do the schools have sixth forms? Or will your child have to transfer at 16 to a college or another school?

Specialist Schools. Some of the schools in your area may specialise. The most obvious are the grammar schools that are likely to have entrance tests to select pupils. Many schools also provide vocational courses as a supplement to the national curriculum. These are an important option at 14, and particularly 16, for children for whom studies related to the world of work would be more enjoyable and fulfilling. Other schools will have developed a particular expertise in areas such as special needs, art, music or sport.

Single Sex or Mixed Schools. A number of areas across the country also have single sex schools. The debate about whether they are better than mixed schools is heated. There is evidence that girls in all-girl schools do benefit in traditionally male-dominated subjects such as mathematics and science. The absence of boys may ensure that they are not deterred from doing well in the subjects.

Independent Schools. Some parents choose to send their child to independent school after state primary school. The attractions are usually smaller classes, firm discipline, good examination results and a wider range of facilities. However, it can be a costly option. Even if you can afford it, it is well worth considering what is available in the state sector where education is free. Many state schools are achieving results on a par with their independent rivals.

A significant number of independent schools do offer financial help through scholarships or bursaries. There is also the government's assisted places scheme. Entry to an independent school may require your child to sit an entrance examination. These examinations may be taken at 11 or 13.

Getting More Information

There are four other main sources of information about secondary schools: prospectuses, the governors' annual report, reports by government inspectors and performance or 'league' tables of examination results.

Prospectuses and Governors' Reports

These can be obtained from the schools. They should contain the same information as those for primary schools, but with additional details on:

- The school's latest examination results for pupils aged 15 and 17 at the start of the school year.

- A list of all the qualifications and courses offered.

- Details of careers education and work experience.

There are also likely to be sections on admissions criteria, school reports, parent–teacher relations, how to apply and how to appeal, extra-curricular activities such as sport, music, art and drama, how the school is organised and school meals.

Governors' annual reports will contain the same information as those for primary schools, although there should also be details of examination results.

School Inspectors' Reports

The new school inspection arrangements introduced by the government will mean that from September 1993 each secondary school will be inspected every four years. To find out whether a school is to be inspected in the next few months or has been inspected recently, you should contact the school, the local education authority or Ofsted, Inspectors' Reports, Elizabeth House, York Road, London SE1 7PH. Tel: 071-925-6742.

Examination Results

Secondary schools' GCSE and A-level results, which are included in their prospectuses and governors' reports, should follow a standard format. The tables can appear complex but they are useful. They should give the examination results for two key age groups:

- Pupils aged 15 at the start of the school year (who sit GCSEs).

- Pupils aged 17 at the start of the school year (who sit A-levels and/or A/S levels).

Other qualifications gained by pupils at the school should also be reported.

Schools should also give information showing how many pupils were not entered for GCSE examinations. Some schools have strict policies about who is entered for particular examinations. Others encourage as many as possible to enter even if they may have only a marginal chance of success.

League Tables

Each November the government publishes tables of GCSE and A-level results for each secondary school in every local education authority area. The tables are generally sent to primary schools, local education authorities, secondary schools and local libraries. The government also proposes to publish separate tables of results to show how 14-year-olds at each school performed in national curriculum tests. The boycott of the tests in 1993 made these tables impossible to compile.

For further information on the distribution and availability of the tables, you should contact the Department for Education's Public Inquiry Unit, Sanctuary Buildings, Great Smith Street, London SW1P 3BT. Tel: 071-925-5000.

'League' tables of an individual school's examination results should be treated with caution even at secondary schools. Those schools which select their pupils for their academic ability will do better than those which don't. The number of pupils who have English as a second language may also influence results. However, there are still schools in similar areas with pupils who have similar backgrounds that produce very different results. It is proof that schools *can* make a difference to how well children do.

In assessing the different results of schools, it is important to compare like with like. A school may be doing well if a child gets C and D grades after starting from a low level of academic achievement. That will not rate highly in a league table, but the school may, in fact, be doing better than another which takes high-flying 11-year-olds who, not surprisingly, go on to get A grades. The other factor is to see whether the results are consistent across different departments in the school. Are some doing substantially better than others?

The final point, however, is to recognise that, although examination results are very important, children can shine in other areas of the curriculum and school life. Choose the school that is best suited to your child's all-round abilities.

Questions to Ask

Here are some questions that are especially relevant to secondary schools:

- Does the school usually get more applications than places?

- Are there additional tests beyond those required in the national curriculum?

- Are children grouped by ability? If so, how is that decided? Is there streaming?

- How is the school organised? Are there form tutors, house or year groups?

- What careers advice is offered?

- What subjects or combinations of subjects are offered at 14 (Key Stage Four)? Are there any vocational, job-related courses? And what subjects beyond those required in the national curriculum?

- Is there adequate equipment and technical assistance for science teaching?

- What are the school's policies on entering pupils for GCSEs and A-levels?

- What A-levels and/or vocational courses are offered?

- What do most pupils do at 16? How many go on to university, further education, training or jobs?

- How big are the classes?

- What is the school's policy on homework, on discipline, on school uniform?

- What extra-curricular activities are offered?

- How involved are parents in the school?

- What are the attendance rates of pupils?

- How stable is the school's staff?

- How does the school cater for children with special talents or educational needs?

Visiting the school is also just as important. All the general points and questions in the section on what to look for in a primary school apply to secondary schools.

How to Appeal If You Are Refused a School Place

Parents have a right to appeal if their child is turned down for a place at their preferred school. If you are rejected, you should be told by the education authority or school governors about your right of appeal and how to use it. The information should also be included in admissions booklets.

You will have a fixed period in which to decide whether to lodge an appeal. You are also likely to be given an alternative school (possibly your second preference) or a list of schools from which you can choose another. If you decide to go to appeal, you should see whether it is possible to reserve a place at another school (possibly your second preference) before that too fills up. You will have to strike an agreement with the education authority that you can do this without prejudicing your appeal.

If you win your case, then the authority or governors have to provide you with a place at the school. If you fail and feel that the procedures have not been properly handled, then you can take matters further. If it is a county school, you can complain to the local government ombudsman. Alternatively, you can complain to the Secretary of State for Education.

Further Information

Useful Addresses

Commission for Local Administration (Local Ombudsman)

England: 21 Queen Anne's Gate, London SW1H 9BU. Tel: 071-222-5622.

Wales: Derwen House, Court Road, Bridgend, Mid Glamorgan CF31 1BN. Tel: 0656-661325.

Department for Education (DFE), Sanctuary Buildings, Great Smith Street, London SW1P 3BT. Tel: 071-925-5000.

Advisory Centre for Education (ACE), 1B Aberdeen Studios, 22 Highbury Grove, London N5 2EA. Free telephone advice line 2–5pm. every weekday – 071-354-8321. (ACE publishes a free two-side leaflet explaining your rights. Also available from ACE is *School Choice and Appeals* (£4.50), a guide to the law with advice on choosing a school and the appeals procedure. A complete list of ACE publications is available free. These offer comprehensive coverage of parents' rights in all aspects of state school education.)

The Grant-Maintained Schools Foundation, 36 Great Smith Street, London SW1P 3BU. Tel: 071-233-4666.

Local Schools Information (LSI), 1st floor, 1–5 Bath Street, London EC1V 9QQ. Tel: 071-490-4942. Advice organisation on grant-maintained schools.

The City Technology Colleges Trust, 15 Young Street, London W8 5EH. Tel: 071-376-2511.

Independent Schools Information Service (ISIS), 56 Buckingham Gate, London SW1E 6AG. Tel: 071-630-8793/4. They publish a book of independent schools and a list of schools that are part of the assisted places scheme.

Further information about the assisted places scheme, including eligibility, is available from:

Assisted Places Team, Department for Education, Mowden Hall, Staindrop Road, Darlington, Co. Durham DL3 9BG. Tel 0325 392156/8.

7
Parents' Rights

The government's 'Parent's Charter' lays down the rights that parents have to information, to a choice of school and to good standards in education. It draws together legislation that has been passed by Parliament and is designed to underpin these rights.

It is part of the 'Citizen's Charter', which aims to guarantee certain basic standards and inform you of your rights. This chapter outlines your rights on education under the legislation.

School Reports

All parents must receive a written report on their child's progress at least once a year. Government regulations lay down a basic minimum amount of information that parents should get. Reports must include:

- Teachers' comments on your child's progress in all the national curriculum subjects.

- Your child's attendance record.

- Comments on your child's general progress – an overall view of how your child is performing academically, your child's behaviour, contribution to school life and any notable achievements in the past year.

- What your child has achieved in other subjects and activities taught during the year.

- The name of a teacher or teachers with whom the report can be discussed and how to fix a time to do so.

Additional information should be provided when pupils reach the end of each Key Stage at seven, 11 and 14, and sit national curriculum tests. This should include details about the levels that your child has reached in the 'core' subjects of English, mathematics and science, with a commentary by teachers to explain what the grades mean.

For GCSE and A-level candidates, parents should receive details of subjects in which their child has gained a certificate, the grades achieved and how their child has done in comparison with other pupils in the same school and nationally. These results may be sent on after the main report. Other qualifications from vocational courses, for example, should also be included. For pupils who have not taken GCSEs in some or any national curriculum subjects, the school must provide information about their performance in those subjects.

Records of Achievement

All school-leavers also have to be issued with standardised records of their work in the classroom and outside. Called National Records of Achievement, pupils can present them to employers or college admissions tutors. As well as GCSE and A-level results, the records list vocational qualifications, non-academic successes in fields such as music or sport, details of work experience, spare-time interests and any voluntary or charitable work. In addition, the records include a pupil's own written assessment of his or her school career, and a reference from teachers.

For an explanation of what the grades and levels mean, see Chapter 5 on tests and examinations.

Who Can See the Reports?

Parents have a right to see school records on their child's progress at any time provided they give 15 days' notice of their request to governors.

Annual Governors' Reports to Parents

Each school's governors have to compile an annual report for discussion at a parents' meeting, which governors have to hold each year. The report must be circulated to parents at least two weeks before the meeting, telling them when it will be held. The report will give you an idea about how the school is doing and any important changes that are being planned.

Annual Parents' Meetings

All parents with pupils registered at school must be invited. Any topic about the work of the school may be discussed at the meeting, although it would be inappropriate to raise issues about individual teachers or pupils.

If enough parents attend (the equivalent of at least 20% of the number of registered pupils at the school), they can vote on resolutions put forward by individual parents. Governors have to consider any resolutions passed by a simple majority vote, and report back to parents.

Inspectors' Reports

A new national inspectorate, called the Office for Standards in Education (OFSTED), has been set up to produce regular reports on all state schools. All secondary schools will be inspected over four years from September 1993. All primary schools will be inspected over four years from September 1994.

The inspectors will hold a meeting with parents during their visit to your school. Once the inspection is completed, they have five weeks in which to submit their report to your school's governors. The governors must send a summary of the report to all parents with details of their plans for tackling any problems. Copies of the full report will be placed in local libraries. Parents have the right to ask the school for the full report, although they may be charged for any photocopying.

Governors must give details of how they are

responding at an annual parents' meeting, while a summary of the inspectors' report may be included in the school's prospectus.

Going Grant-Maintained?

Grant-maintained schools were created by the Education Reform Act of 1988. They are schools that have 'opted out' of local education authority control and receive their funds direct from the government.

The education that they provide is still free, they are still state schools and they must still follow the national curriculum. Some 4% of the 24,000 primary and secondary schools have so far gone grant-maintained. However, it is certain that in the next few years many other schools will discuss whether to join them.

A proposal to opt out can only be submitted to the Secretary of State for Education after parents have had the chance to vote on it in a secret ballot. There must be a majority vote in favour for the application to be considered by the minister. A ballot of parents can be prompted in two ways: either the governors can put the proposal to parents after passing a resolution at one of their meetings, or more than 20% of parents can draw up a petition requesting a ballot.

One of the incentives for becoming grant-maintained has been the extra funds that the school gets. Local authorities hold back a certain amount of money for centrally-provided services such as advisory teachers or music centres. It is usually no more than 15% of the school's budget. Grant-maintained schools receive these extra funds and are free to use them in ways that they feel may be more appropriate.

They are also free to decide their own admissions policies. However, any change that would affect the character of the school (such as becoming selective) can only be done after consultation with parents and with the approval of the Secretary of State.

The Right to Complain

Most parents and their children will go through school without experiencing the kind of problems that require a formal complaint. It may well be possible to sort out any difficulties through informal discussions with your child's class teacher or with the head teacher. However, there are established procedures if you wish to take matters further.

When taking such action, you should try to support your case with factual evidence rather than hearsay and know the procedures so that you can be sure that you are lodging your complaint with the right body.

On most issues, your complaint will be considered initially by the governors. They are responsible for managing the school effectively, ensuring that the national curriculum is followed, appointing, disciplining and dismissing staff, and deciding how to spend the school budget. The governors should have established procedures to deal with complaints about any of these issues, as well as about matters such as discipline and charging parents for activities.

If you remain dissatisfied, you can complain to the local education authority, where the director of education (sometimes described as the chief education officer) has overall responsibility. It, too, will have an established mechanism for dealing with complaints. If your school is grant-maintained, you should take your complaint to the Department for Education.

If you are still dissatisfied, you can complain to the Secretary of State for Education. And, if you are unhappy with the way the case has been handled by the education authority or by a government department, you can go the appropriate independent watchdog body:

- The Commission for Local Administration (the local ombudsman) deals with complaints against local authorities.

- The Parliamentary Commissioner for Administration (the parliamentary ombudsman) deals with complaints against government departments.

If you are unhappy about the way that complaints over sexual or racial discrimination have been handled by a school or local education authority, you should contact the Equal Opportunities Commission or the Commission for Racial Equality. Schools should have published policies on equal opportunities and racial equality.

Expulsions from School

Expulsions are known as 'exclusions'. Pupils can be excluded from a school for fixed periods of time or permanently, depending on the seriousness of the breach of its rules on behaviour.

If your child is excluded, the head teacher must inform you without delay and give the reasons for the decision. If your child is suspended for a fixed period, the head teacher should also tell you when your child will be allowed back into school. You have a right to make representations to the governors and your local education authority. You should be told about the procedures when your child is excluded.

If your child is excluded permanently and the decision has been supported by the governors and local education authority, you have a right to take your case to an appeals committee. The local authority must inform you of that right.

Only permanent exclusion leads to the removal of a pupil from a school's roll. The local education authority has to ensure that another school is found for the child. Parents have a right to choose an alternative school and that preference must be complied with unless the school is already full.

More than 3000 pupils are excluded permanently from school each year. Aggression against other pupils and disobedience are the most common reasons.

Charging

Many schools charge parents for some out-of-school activities. They are known as 'optional extras' and the school's policy on charging must be published in its prospectus. There are, however, official guidelines laid down that define the activities that schools can and cannot charge to parents.

The fundamentals must remain free: no charges can be made for admitting pupils, or for education or activities offered during the school day including books, equipment and transport. There is only one exception: schools can charge for teaching pupils to play a musical instrument. But even this is not allowed if it is an essential part of the national curriculum or a set examination syllabus. Some schools still offer tuition free of charge.

Schools can charge for:

- Board and lodging on school trips. This excludes families on income support and family credit.

- Out-of-school activities that are not part of the national curriculum, if parents agree.

- Repayment of public examination entry fees if a pupil fails to take an examination without good reason or was not prepared for the examination by the school.

- A re-check of public examination results where requested by parents.

- Ingredients/materials for practical subjects where parents or the child say they want to keep the finished product.

- Contributions towards damage or loss of equipment or books caused by a pupil's behaviour.

Benefits

Children of parents who are receiving income support are entitled to free school meals. Some local education authorities and school governors also provide grants for school uniforms, although the number is declining.

Education authorities must provide free transport to school where it is not within walking distance of the child's home (two miles for a child under eight, three miles for a child over eight). Some authorities provide free transport under those distances if they feel it is appropriate.

For further information about your entitlement to support, you should contact your local citizens' advice bureau, social security offices, local education authority and possibly your school.

Religious Education and Acts of Collective Worship

All state schools must provide religious education (RE) and daily collective worship for all pupils up to the age of 18.

The 1988 Education Reform Act states that RE should 'reflect the fact that the religious traditions are in the main Christian', while taking account of the practices of the other principal religions represented in Britain. This wording has caused some confusion. However, many government advisers believe that schools should devote at least half of their teaching time in RE to Christianity.

The school's syllabus has to be based on guidelines drawn up by a local Standing Advisory Council for Religious Education (SACRE), a body of local church leaders, local council representatives and teachers. The SACRE is set up by the local education authority, which should have details about its membership and syllabus.

Schools can apply to the SACRE to exempt some or all of their pupils from the requirement to be taught 'mainly Christian' RE if they feel that it is inappropriate for children from different religious groups. Voluntary church schools can teach a different RE syllabus according to their denomination.

Daily collective worship can be held at any time during the day and does not have to involve the entire school at once. Worship has to be 'broadly Christian' unless the school has got an exemption from the SACRE.

Parents have a right to withdraw their child from RE and collective worship. However, you should speak to your school first and establish what alternative arrangements can be made if you want your child to be taught in accordance with your own faith. Schools will have complaints procedures if you are dissatisfied with either RE or collective worship.

Many authorities have not yet adopted new syllabuses to meet the requirements of the 1988 Act. New legislation, introduced in 1993, gives them a one-year deadline to do so.

Further Information

The Department for Education (DFE) publishes booklets for parents on the curriculum, examinations and tests, vocational qualifications, your rights, grant-maintained schools, special needs and choosing a school. The booklets and copies of The Parent's Charter should be available at local authorities, schools or libraries. Or contact the Public Inquiries Unit, Department for Education, Sanctuary Buildings, Great Smith Street, London SW1P 3BT. Tel: 071-925-5000.

Advisory Centre for Education (ACE), 1B Aberdeen Studios, 22 Highbury Grove, London N5 2EA. Free telephone advice line 2–5 pm. every weekday – 071-354-8321. ACE publishes leaflets explaining your rights on information and complaints procedures. Also available is their *Parents' Information Checklist* (£4.50).

Commission for Local Administration (Local Ombudsman)

England: 21 Queen Anne's Gate, London SW1H 9BU. Tel: 071-222-5622.

Wales: Derwen House, Court Road, Bridgend, Mid Glamorgan CF31 1BN. Tel: 0656-661325.

The Parliamentary Commissioner for Administration (Parliamentary Ombudsman), Church House, Great Smith Street, London SW1P 3BW. Tel: 071-276-2130. Complaints will only be investigated if they are submitted to the commissioner by an MP.

Equal Opportunities Commission, Overseas House, Quay Street, Manchester M3 3HN. Tel: 061-833-9244.

Commission for Racial Equality, Elliot House, 10/12 Allington Street, London SW1E 5EH. Tel: 071-828-7022.

National Confederation of Parent–Teacher Associations (NCPTA), 2 Ebbsfleet Industrial Estate, Stonebridge Road, Gravesend, Kent DA11 9DZ. Tel: 0474-560618.

National Association of Governors and Managers, 21 Bennets Hill, Birmingham B2 5QP. Tel: 021-643-5787.

8
Special Options

Children with Special Educational Needs

Children are entitled to special support at school if they have particular difficulties. These include physical disabilities, emotional or behavioural problems, or specific difficulties with their school work or aspects of the curriculum.

If your child is having problems, you should consult your child's teacher and the head teacher. The problems could be sorted out without any further action. Many schools will be able to provide extra help; some employ teachers with the specialist expertise to help your child.

However, you can go further and ask your local education authority to make a formal assessment of your child's special educational needs. The aim of this procedure is to secure a 'statement' of a child's special needs.

This statement lays down what support your child must receive. That might include an additional teacher in the classroom, a place at a special school, lessons in a separate unit or even help with fees to send the child to an independent school. There are about 168,000 pupils with statements of special needs, amounting to some 2% of all schoolchildren. Many are physically or mentally handicapped. Some have learning disorders such as dyslexia.

The local education authority must meet your request for an assessment unless they can show that it is unreasonable. Your head teacher can also request an assessment. School governors have to ensure that your child receives the extra help specified in the statement, if the assessment leads to one. Local education authorities are responsible for all children with special educational needs in all schools in their area, including those that are grant-maintained.

Parents have rights to appeal if they disagree with the terms of the statement.

If you need advice or information, you should contact one of the following organisations who have expertise in special needs:

- The Department for Education, Sanctuary Buildings, Great Smith Street, London SW1P 3BT. Tel: 071-925-5000.

- Advisory Centre for Education (ACE), 1B Aberdeen Studios, 22 Highbury Grove, London N5 2EA. Free telephone advice line 2–5 pm. every weekday: 071-354-8321.

- Independent Panel for Special Education Advice, 12 Marsh Road, Tillingham, Essex, CM0 7SZ. Tel: 0621-779781 or 0628-478986.

Music

The national curriculum lays down the basic musical skills and knowledge that pupils should have been taught by the ages of seven, 11 and 14. From the age of 14, music is optional.

Here are some examples of what your child should be able to do:

At Age Seven

- Sing a familiar song; repeat the rhythm clapped by a teacher

- Sing in a group and play simple instruments such as a single chord on a piano.

- Write a simple graphic score for a piece they have composed.

- Listen and respond to short pieces of music in different styles and explain the differences.

At Age 11

- Perform from a simple score.

- Sing and play a range of music, controlling pitch and rhythm.

- Use recorders, keyboards, computers and electronic equipment when composing.

- Undertake simple analysis and evaluation of musical compositions and performances.

At Age 14

- Perform in a range of styles, interpreting signs, symbols and musical instructions.

- Perform a solo part on a musical instrument with fluency and expression.

- Take part in group performances (vocal, instrumental or mixed), and know when to take the lead and when to accompany others.

Extra Help for Music

The quality of music teaching offered by schools will vary widely depending on their facilities, staffing and priorities. It is important to choose your school carefully if you feel that your child has a particular interest in the subject.

A number of local education authorities have music centres for use by teachers and pupils. These may offer instrumental tuition, choral singing and orchestral and group playing. Many authorities also still employ specialist advisers and teachers of music who might be able to help with advice, although spending cuts have reduced their numbers. Full details for each local authority are published in *The Music Teachers' Year Book*, which is generally available in local libraries. Another option is to pay for a private music teacher.

Registers of music teachers, consultants and advisers are published by the Incorporated Society of Musicians (ISM).

Special grants or scholarships are available for talented young musicians to study at fee-paying schools or colleges. They are offered by specialist music schools, independent schools, choir schools, some trusts and some charities. A number of independent schools, choir schools and specialist music schools also offer subsidised places under the government's Assisted Places Scheme. *The Music Teachers' Year Book* contains details of awards available.

Decisions about a career in music should be taken in consultation with your child's music and careers teachers. ISM also publish a guide to careers in music.

Further information about music education can be obtained from:

Incorporated Society of Musicians, 10 Stratford Place, London W1N 9AE. Tel: 071-629-4413.

Associated Board of the Royal Schools of Music, 14 Bedford Square, London WC1B 3JG. Tel: 071-636-5400. (It organises examinations in practical instruments and musical theory for all grades.)

Assisted Places Scheme Team, Department for Education, Mowden Hall, Staindrop Road, Darlington, Co. Durham DL3 9BG. Tel: 0325 392156/8.

The Music Teachers' Year Book, Rhinegold Publishing Ltd, 241 Shaftesbury Avenue, London WC2H 8EH. Tel: 071-240-5749.

Art

The national curriculum lays down the basic skills and knowledge in art that pupils should have been taught by seven, 11 and 14. From the age of 14, art is optional.

Here are some examples of what your child should be able to do:

At Age Seven

- Draw or paint a large picture based on a favourite story or piece of music.

- Collect and sort images and objects (eg. different coloured pebbles) and use them as a basis for their work.

- Recognise different kinds of art at home or on visits (eg. illustrations in books, toys or paintings in galleries).

At Age 11

- Make carefully observed drawings around the school (eg. from looking through a window or an imaginary bird's-eye view).

- Experiment with different ways of printing the same image (eg. sponge rollers and stencils, hard rollers and polystyrene or card blocks).

- Identify different kinds of art and their purposes.

At Age 14

- Record examples of towers, spires and pylons in their area before doing a design-based project (eg. a printed textile).

- Design and print a poster to make people aware of an issue of public concern.

- Apply imaginatively the methods and approaches of other artists in presenting their own ideas and feelings.

Extra Help for Art

There are just as wide variations in the standard of art education in schools as in music teaching. If your child is interested or talented in art, you should be prepared to look around several different schools.

Good schools will take pupils on regular visits to galleries, museums, arts centres, festivals, theatres or dance events, and organise out-of-school activities. To find out what might be available in your area, you should contact the Regional Arts Associations or Boards and your local authority.

For further information about arts activities contact the **Regional Arts Associations** whose details are available from the **Arts Council**, 14 Great Peter Street, London SW1P 3NQ. Tel: 071-333-0100.

For further information about courses and careers in art, design and technology, contact The **Design Council**, 28 Haymarket, London SW1Y 4SU. Tel: 071-839-8000.

You can also contact the **Art and Design Admissions Registry** (which organises applications to most degree courses), Penn House, 9 Broad Street, Hereford HR4 9AP. Tel: 0432-266653.

Physical Education and Sport

Out-of-school sports activities have declined in recent years, forcing many parents to look outside school to leisure centres and local sports clubs.

The national curriculum in physical education is an ambitious attempt to reverse the decline. Although it includes 'sports', it also aims to teach children the importance of an active and healthy lifestyle. It is not designed to create a nation of super-athletes. Rather, it aims to help children learn key basic skills in six activities: athletics, dance, games, gymnastics, outdoor education and swimming. If a child is keen on sport, you should be prepared to look around a number of schools to find out the variety of sports offered, the standard of facilities and staffing qualifications.

Pupils should do all six activities in the PE curriculum until the age of 11. Swimming can be taught at either Key Stage One (five to seven) or Key Stage Two (seven to 11). From 11 to 14, children have to do games and at least three other activities. From 14 to 16, those pupils not doing a GCSE in physical education have to study at least two activities.

Here are some examples of what children will be expected to do in physical education:

At Age Seven

- Recognise and work within simple rules such as the Green Cross Code.

- Practise, perform and develop simple skills such as different ways of sending, receiving and travelling with a ball.

- Recognise the effects of physical exercise such as breathing more rapidly.

At Age 11

- Swim unaided for 25 metres and be taught water safety.

- Plan, practise and remember more complex sequences of movements such as those in a simple group dance.

- Understand the effects of exercise on the body.

At Age 14

- Work out tactics to outwit opponents such as deciding the order in a relay race.

- Plan and perform dance routines.

- Plan simple and safe health-related activities such as monitoring heart rate and recovery after a middle distance event.

Children will not be tested in PE in the same way as other subjects, although some schools offer GCSEs in physical education. Full details of the syllabuses should be available in your school.

Further information can be obtained from:

The Sports Council, 16 Upper Woburn Place, London WC1H 0QP. Tel: 071-388-1277.

Central Council of Physical Recreation, Francis House, Francis Street, London SW1P 1DE. Tel: 071-828-3163.

Technology

The government's attempts to improve the quality of technology teaching have included grants to about 200 schools to improve their facilities. There are also 15 City Technology Colleges in urban areas around the country, specialising in the teaching of technology.

The government's Education Act of 1993 also allows for the creation of grant-maintained technology colleges. These will be schools that have opted out of local authority control and which then link up with business sponsors to provide a curriculum with a special emphasis on technology.

For further information, you can contact:

The City Technology Colleges Trust, 15 Young Street, London W8 5EH. Tel: 071-376-2511.

Specialist State Schools

Legislative changes announced by the government allow all state schools to select up to 10% of their pupils for their abilities in music, art, physical education or technology. The aim is to help create specialist schools.

Any school intending to select pupils in these subjects should explain to prospective parents what they offer and how they plan to choose children. This information should be included in the school's prospectus.

What Can I Do If My Child Is Very Able Or Gifted?

There are six areas where a child can show high ability.

- Academic achievement in one or more subjects.

- Great talent in one or more of the arts (music, painting, drama).

- Exceptional physical abilities or games skills

- Practical or mechanical ingenuity.

- Social leadership.

- Creatively gifted.

One of the most important points is actually to identify whether a child is particularly able in one or some of these areas. Only then can parents and teachers ensure that the child achieves his or her potential. There are two key organisations that provide advice:

The National Association for Gifted Children (NAGC) offers guidance and counselling for parents and teachers. It has a network of 40 branches across the UK which provide support, may put on special activities and enable parents of gifted children to meet. The association may also give you details about residential courses, local events, out-of-school classes for children and seminars. It can also advise you about assessments of your child's abilities.

The National Association for Able Children in Education (NACE) provides support and advice for teachers in teaching able pupils.

If your child is particularly able, your first port of call is his or her school and its teachers. Some local education authorities have advisers and special activities for the more able. Your authority or the two associations above should be able to provide details.

For further information, you can contact:

National Association for Gifted Children (NAGC), Park Campus, Boughton Green Road, Northampton NN2 7AL. Tel: 0604-792300.

National Association for Able Children in Education (NACE) (same address as for NAGC).

Reading Lists for English

Key Stage One
(children aged five to seven)

Nursery rhymes: Examples include 'London Bridge is Falling Down',' Oranges and Lemons', poetry chosen from anthologies like *Singing in the Sun*, edited by Jill Bennett, *Poems for Seven Year Olds and Under*, edited by Helen Nicoll, and poems from collections by individual poets, eg. *Complete Poems for Children* by James Reeves, *Hot Dog and Other Poems* by Kit Wright, *Come On Into My Tropical Garden* by Grace Nichols.

Poems and stories with settings based on imaginary or fantasy worlds. Examples include *Rosie's Walk* by Pat Hutchins; *But Martin!* by June Counsel; *The Elephant and the Bad Baby* by Elfrida Vipont and Raymond Briggs.

Books and poems by significant children's authors. Examples include Janet and Allan Ahlberg (*Each Peach Pear Plum*); John Burningham (*Mr Gumpy's Outing*); Maurice Sendak (*Where the Wild Things Are*); Eric Carle (*The Very Hungry Caterpillar*); Pat Hutchins (*Titch*); Shirley Hughes (*Dogger*); Jill Tomlinson (*The Owl Who Was Afraid of the Dark*); Anthony Browne (*Bear Hunt*); David McKee (*Not Now, Bernard*); Dick King-Smith (*Lady Daisy*); Beatrix Potter (*The Tale of Peter Rabbit*); Alison Uttley (*Little Grey Rabbit to the Rescue*).

Traditional stories, folk and fairy stories, such as *Popular Folk Tales by the Brothers Grimm* (translated by Brian Alderson), *Rapunzel*, retold by Barbara Rogasky, and Bible stories in a modern or simplified version.

Stories from other cultures, such as *Katie Morag Delivers the Mail* by Mairi Hedderwick; *A Story, A Story*, retold by Gail E. Haley; *Nini at Carnival* by Errol Lloyd.

More challenging works, such as *The Iron Man* by Ted Hughes; *A Necklace of Raindrops* by Joan Aiken; *The Just So Stories* by Rudyard Kipling.

Key Stage Two
(children aged seven to 11)

Verses by writers such as: Kit Wright, Ogden Nash, Brian Patten, James Reeves, Charles Causley, Michael Rosen, Ted Hughes, John Agard, Grace Nichols, Allan Ahlberg, Gareth Owen; material drawn from anthologies such as *A Third Poetry Book*, edited by John Foster; *The Golden Treasury of Poetry*, edited by Louis Untermeyer; *A Child's Garden of Verses*, edited by R.L. Stevenson; *Poems for Over Ten-Year-Olds*, edited by Kit Wright.

Fiction by writers such as: Ian Serraillier, E. B. White, Betsy Byars, Rumer Godden, Gene Kemp, Russell Hoban, Rosemary Sutcliff, Jenny Nimmo, Dick King-Smith, Joan Aiken, T.H. White, Leon Garfield, Susan Cooper, Philippa Pearce, Richard Adams, Clive King, Jill Paton Walsh, Alan Garner, Judith Kerr, Roald Dahl, Jill Murphy, Helen Cresswell.

Classic poetry such as: John Masefield, 'Sea Fever'; H.W. Longfellow, 'The Wreck of the Hesperus'; Edward Lear, 'The Jumblies'; Walter de la Mare, 'The Listeners'; Lewis Carroll, 'You are Old, Father William'; T.S. Eliot, 'Macavity, the Mystery Cat'; Alfred Noyes, 'The Highwayman'; Eleanor Farjeon, 'It Was Long Ago'; Hilaire Belloc, 'Tarantella'.

Long-established children's fiction, such as Lewis Carroll (*Alice's Adventures in Wonderland*); J.M. Barrie (*Peter Pan*); Richmal Crompton (*Just William*); Arthur Ransome (*Swallows and Amazons*); Kenneth Grahame (*The Wind in the Willows*); C.S. Lewis (*The Lion, the Witch and the Wardrobe*); A.A. Milne (*Winnie the Pooh*); Rudyard Kipling (*The Jungle Book*); E. Nesbit (*The Railway Children*); Laura Ingalls Wilder (*The Little House on the Prairie*); Susan Coolidge (*What Katy Did*); Mary Norton (*The Borrowers*).

Texts from other cultures and traditions, such as Valerie Flournoy (*The Patchwork Quilt*); Anita Desai (*The Village by the Sea*); Madhur Jaffrey (*Seasons of Splendour*).

Myths, legends and traditional stories, such as *The Faber Book of Greek Legends*, edited by Kathleen Lines; *Book of British Fairy Tales*, edited by Alan Garner; *The Broonie, Silkies and Fairies*; *Travellers' Tales* by Duncan Williamson; *Mouth Open, Story Jump Out* by Grace Hallworth.

Texts to broaden perspectives and encourage imagination, such as T.H. White (*The Once and Future King*); Gwyn Thomas and Kevin Crossley-Holland (*Tales from the Mabinogion*); Ted Hughes (*How the Whale Became*); Joan Aiken (*The Wolves of Willoughby Chase*); Rosemary Sutcliff (*Warrior Scarlet*); J.R.R. Tolkien (*The Hobbit*); Lewis Carroll (*Jabberwocky* and *Stories from the Bible*); Helen Cresswell (*The Piemakers*).

Texts with more complex narrative, such as Betsy Byars (*The Eighteenth Emergency*); Alan Garner (*Tom Fobble's Day*); Penelope Lively (*The Ghost of Thomas Kempe*); Philippa Pearce (*Tom's Midnight Garden*); Catherine Storr (*Clever Polly and the Stupid Wolf*); Jill Murphy (*On the Way Home*); Ted Hughes (*The Iron Man*); Gene Kemp (*The Turbulent Term of Tyke Tiler*); Paul Theroux (*A Christmas Card*); Janet and Allan Ahlberg (*The Jolly Postman: or Other People's Letters*); Anthony Browne (*Gorilla*); Florence Parry Heide (*The Shrinking of Treehorn*); Jenny Nimmo (*The Snow

Spider); Michael Foreman (*Dinosaurs and all that Rubbish*); Robert Browning (*The Pied Piper of Hamelin*).

Figurative language in poetry and prose, such as Alan Garner (*The Stone Book*); Emily Brontë (*All Hushed and Still Within the House*); Jenny Wagner (*John Brown, Rose and the Midnight Cat*); Russell Hoban (*How Tom Beat Captain Najork and His Hired Sportsmen*); Antonia Barber and Nicola Bayley (*The Mousehole Cat*).

Key Stage Three
(examples of literature for pupils aged 11 to 14)

Plays such as *Under Milk Wood* by Dylan Thomas; *Pygmalion* by G.B. Shaw; *The Granny Project* by A. Fine; *Roses of Eyam* by D. Taylor.

Fiction by authors such as R.L. Stevenson (*Treasure Island*); Mark Twain (*Adventures of Huckleberry Finn*); L.M. Alcott (*Little Women*); Daniel Defoe (*Robinson Crusoe*); Thomas Hardy (*Wessex Tales*); Charlotte Brontë (*Jane Eyre*); Charles Dickens (*A Christmas Carol*); George Orwell, Stan Barstow, John Steinbeck, H.G. Wells, H.E. Bates, William Golding, J.R.R. Tolkien, Nina Bawden, Alan Garner, Leon Garfield, Rosemary Sutcliff, Ursula Le Guin, Penelope Lively, Jan Mark, Rukshana Smith, Michelle Margorian, Beverley Naidoo, Anne Holm, Berlie Doherty, Joan Lingard, Katherine Paterson, Philippa Pearce, Rosa Guy, Marjorie Darke, Gwyn Thomas.

Works by poets such as Seamus Heaney, Ted Hughes, W.H. Auden, T.S. Eliot, Robert Graves, R.S. Thomas, D.H. Lawrence, Siegfried Sassoon, Dylan Thomas, Grace Nichols, Gillian Clarke, Vernon Scannell, Edwin Muir, Elizabeth Jennings, Charles Causley, John Betjeman, Leslie Norris, Wendy Cope, James Berry, Anne Stevenson, William Blake, S.T. Coleridge, Thomas Hardy, Robert Browning, John Keats, Alfred Lord Tennyson, Emily Dickinson.

Key Stage Four
(examples of literature for pupils aged 14 to 16)

Drama by playwrights such as Harold Brighouse, Arthur Miller, Bill Naughton, J.B. Priestley, G.B. Shaw, R.B. Sheridan, Arnold Wesker, Thornton Wilder, Oliver Goldsmith, R.C. Sherriff, George Farquhar, Oscar Wilde, Robert Bolt, Peter Schaffer, Sean O'Casey, J.M. Synge, Tom Stoppard, Alan Bennett, Henrik Ibsen.

Fiction by authors such as Jonathan Swift (*Gulliver's Travels*); George Eliot (*Silas Marner*); Charles Dickens (*A Tale of Two Cities*); Thomas Hardy (*The Mayor of Casterbridge*); Emily Brontë (*Wuthering Heights*); Jane Austen (*Pride and Prejudice*); Wilkie Collins (*The Moonstone*); Stephen Crane (*The Red Badge of Courage*); Graham Greene, D.H. Lawrence, H.G. Wells, H.E. Bates, William Golding, George Orwell, L.P. Hartley, John Steinbeck, Aldous Huxley, Ernest Hemingway, Harper Lee, Laurie Lee, Ray Bradbury, Somerset Maugham, Evelyn Waugh, Mildred Taylor, John Wyndham, Doris Lessing, Susan Hill, Joseph Conrad, E.M. Forster, Richard Hughes, Winifred Holtby, Alexander Solzhenitsyn.

Works by poets such as William Blake, S.T. Coleridge, Thomas Gray, Alfred Lord Tennyson, William Wordsworth, John Keats, Percy Bysshe Shelley, Robert Herrick, Matthew Arnold, Robert Burns, Robert Bridges, Christina Rossetti, George Herbert, John Donne, Emily Dickinson, Geoffrey Chaucer, John Clare, Robert Frost, Seamus Heaney, Philip Larkin, Wilfred Owen, R.S. Thomas, W.H. Auden, W.B. Yeats, T.S. Eliot, Louis MacNeice, Brian Patten, Derek Walcott, Sylvia Plath, Dannie Abse, Norman MacCaig, Edward Thomas.

Glossary

The following list explains some of the most commonly used terms in schools and colleges. Education is more guilty than many other professions of producing a vocabulary and array of acronyms that is at best complex and at worst impenetrable.

A-level Officially known as Advanced level. An academic examination generally taken by pupils aged 17 or over.

A/S level Advanced Supplementary level. Examination that should take half the time of an A-level but is of equal difficulty.

APS Assisted Places Scheme. Government scheme under which able pupils receive financial help with fees at independent schools.

ATL Association of Teachers and Lecturers. Traditionally moderate teaching union.

Attainment Targets (ATs) Topics within each national curriculum subject (eg. reading, writing, and speaking and listening in English).

Baker Days Training days for teachers during the school year. Named after Kenneth Baker, a former education secretary.

Banding Placing pupils of similar abilities in the same teaching group.

BTEC	Business and Technology Education Council. Body awarding vocational qualifications.		and citizenship.
		CTCs	City Technology Colleges. A new type of school specialising in science and technology education.
CAAW	Curriculum and Assessment Authority for Wales. New body to oversee curriculum and testing in Wales. Takes over from Curriculum Council for Wales (CCW).	DFE	Department for Education. Formerly Department for Education and Science (DES).
C&G	City and Guilds of London Institute. Body awarding vocational qualifications.	Eleven-plus	Popular term for entrance examination for grammar schools, which select pupils by ability.
Catchment Area	The area from which a school would normally expect to draw its pupils.	ERA	Education Reform Act 1988.
		ESL	English as a second language. Extra support may be available for pupils whose language at home is not English.
CDT	Craft, Design and Technology. Now incorporated into technology curriculum.		
CEO	Chief Education Officer. Also known as director of education. The local authority officer in charge of education.	ESW	Education Social Workers. Also known as Education Welfare Officers (EWOs). They oversee the attendance and non-attendance of pupils at school.
Compacts	Formal schemes linking schools and industry. Includes work experience for pupils.	Exclusions	Suspension or expulsion of pupils from school for misbehaviour. Exclusions can be for a fixed period or permanent.
Core Subjects	Mathematics, English, Science and, for schools in Wales which are Welsh-speaking, Welsh.	FE	Further Education. Colleges offering wide range of A-levels and vocational courses, full-time and part-time. Now independent from local education authorities.
Corporal Punishment	Banned in state schools since 1987.		
CPVE	Certificate of Pre-Vocational Education. Broad vocational qualification being replaced by the Diploma of Vocational Education.	Foundation Subjects	Technology, history, geography, modern foreign language, art, music and physical education (plus Welsh in English-speaking schools in Wales).
Cross-curricular themes	Common topics that are often taught across subjects, eg. health, education, environmental education	GCSE	General Certificate of Secondary Education. National examination

	generally taken by pupils aged 15 or over. Replaced O-levels and CSEs.	ITT	Initial Teacher Training. College and school-based courses for students training to be teachers.
GEST	Grants for Education Support and Training. Previously known as Education Support Grants (ESG). Government money earmarked for specific purpose.	Key Stages (KS)	The four phases in children's education, which are completed at the ages of seven, 11, 14 and 16.
		LEAs	Local education authorities. There are 109 in England, eight in Wales and 12 in Scotland.
GM	Grant Maintained schools have opted out of local authority control and receive their funds direct from the government.	Levels of Attainment	The 10 levels (or grades) of attainment for each subject and topic. Pupils progress up the levels. Level one is the lowest; level 10 is achieved only by the brightest children.
GNVQ	General National Vocational Qualification. New national system of vocational qualifications in schools.		
HE	Higher Education. Generally education beyond A-levels. Encompasses 'old' universities, 'new' universities (formerly polytechnics) and colleges of higher education.	LMS	Local Management of Schools. Government reform under which schools and their governors are given control over their own budgets.
		Mixed Ability	Classes where children of differing abilities are taught together.
HMI	Her Majesty's Inspectorate of schools. Now replaced by the Office for Standards in Education (OFSTED).	Mixed Age	Classes where children of different ages are taught together.
		NAGM	National Association of Governors and Managers.
HMSO	Her Majesty's Stationery Office. Publishes government reports.	NAHT	National Association of Head Teachers. Biggest head teachers' and deputy heads' association. Strong in primary schools.
ILEA	Inner London Education Authority. Abolished in 1990.		
INSET	In-service training for teachers during their school careers.	NAS/UWT	National Association of Schoolmasters/Union of Women Teachers. Teaching union with strong representation in secondary schools.
ISIS	Independent Schools Information Service.		
IT	Information Technology (learning how to use computers).		

NCC	National Curriculum Council. Body that oversaw curriculum. To be replaced by School Curriculum and Assessment Authority (SCAA) from October 1993.		provision for pupils.
		PSE	Personal and Social Education. A self-contained subject in some schools, or a cross-curricular theme.
NCPTA	National Confederation of Parent–Teacher Associations.	**PTAs**	Parent–Teacher Associations.
NCVQ	National Council for Vocational Qualifications. Body overseeing introduction of new national system of vocational qualifications.	**PTR**	Pupil-teacher ratio. The ratio of teachers to pupils in a school. Not the same as class size since some teachers may not actually teach or have assigned classes.
NUT	National Union of Teachers. Biggest teaching union with largest representation in primary schools.	**RE**	Religious Education.
		Records of Achievement	Standardised reports for school-leavers, giving details of all qualifications and other achievements.
OFSTED	Office for Standards in Education. New inspectorate that will oversee inspection of schools. Replaced Her Majesty's Inspectorate of schools (HMI).		
		RSA	RSA Examinations Board. Body awarding vocational qualifications.
Open Enrolment	Rules governing admission to schools, which mean that local education authorities and schools cannot limit their intakes of pupils if the schools have the physical capacity to take them.	**SACRE**	Standing Advisory Council for Religious Education. Body set up by local education authority to draw up its RE syllabus.
		SATs	Standard Assessment Tasks. National tests or tasks taken by all children at seven, 11 and 14.
PAT	Professional Association of Teachers. No-strike teaching union.	**SCAA**	School Curriculum and Assessment Authority. New body that will oversee curriculum, testing and examinations from October 1993.
PC	Profile Component. Broad grouping of topics within a national curriculum subject.		
PE	Physical Education.	**SEAC**	School Examinations and Assessment Council. Oversaw testing and exams. To be replaced by School Curriculum and Assessment Authority (SCAA) in October 1993.
Programmes of Study	Syllabuses that lay down what pupils must be taught during each key stage of their education.		
Prospectus	Brochure giving details of a school's courses, facilities and other		

SEN	Special Educational Needs. Pupils can get statements laying down the special education and support that they must receive.	**UCAC**	Undeb Cenedlaethol Athrawon Cymru (National Association of the Teachers of Wales). Welsh-speaking teaching union.
Setting	Grouping pupils of similar abilities in sets according to their skills in particular subjects.	**UCAS**	Universities and Colleges Admissions Service. Body that processes applications for universities and colleges. Formed from merger of Universities Central Council on Admissions (UCCA) and Polytechnics Central Admissions System (PCAS).
SHA	Secondary Heads Association. Represents heads and deputies in secondary sector.		
SoAs	Statements of Attainment. Specific classroom targets that detail the knowledge and skills that pupils should learn and on which they will be tested.	**YT**	Youth Training.
Streaming	Placing pupils of similar abilities in the same group so that they are taught all their subjects together.		
TA	Teacher assessment. Assessment of pupils' performance undertaken by teachers as part of their day-to-day classroom work.		
TECs	Training and Enterprise Councils. Employer-led consortia responsible for youth training.		
TSI	Technology Schools Initiative. Government scheme to enable schools to specialise in technology education.		
TVEI	Technical and Vocational Education Initiative. Nationwide scheme to help develop job-related skills among secondary schoolchildren. Now expanded and known in many schools as TVEE (Technical and Vocational Education Extension).		